A COLLECTION OF ORIGINAL SKETCHES AND ILLUSTRATIONS CREATED BY ARTIST MAHMUD "MUDDY" SUWWAN DURING 2019.

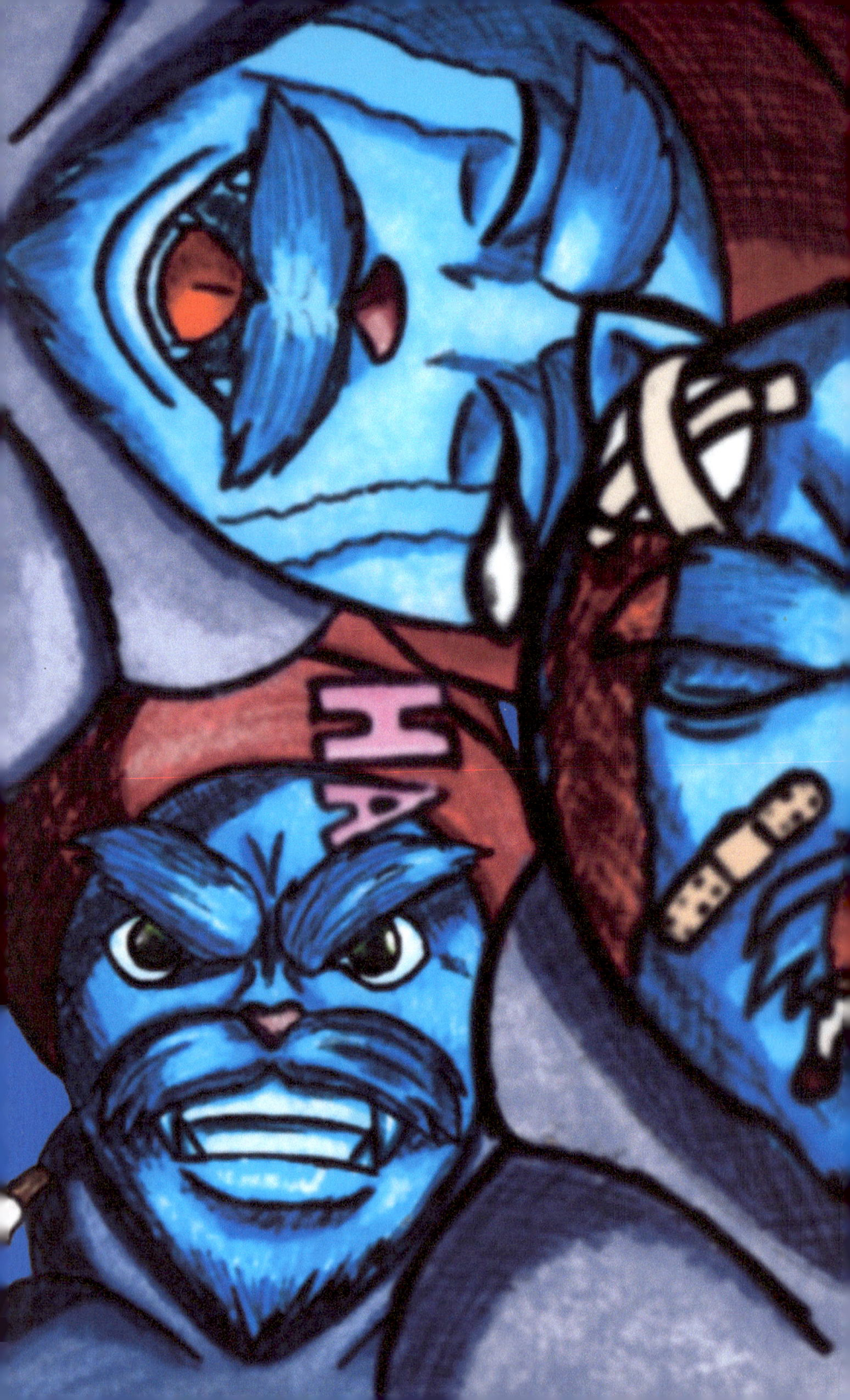

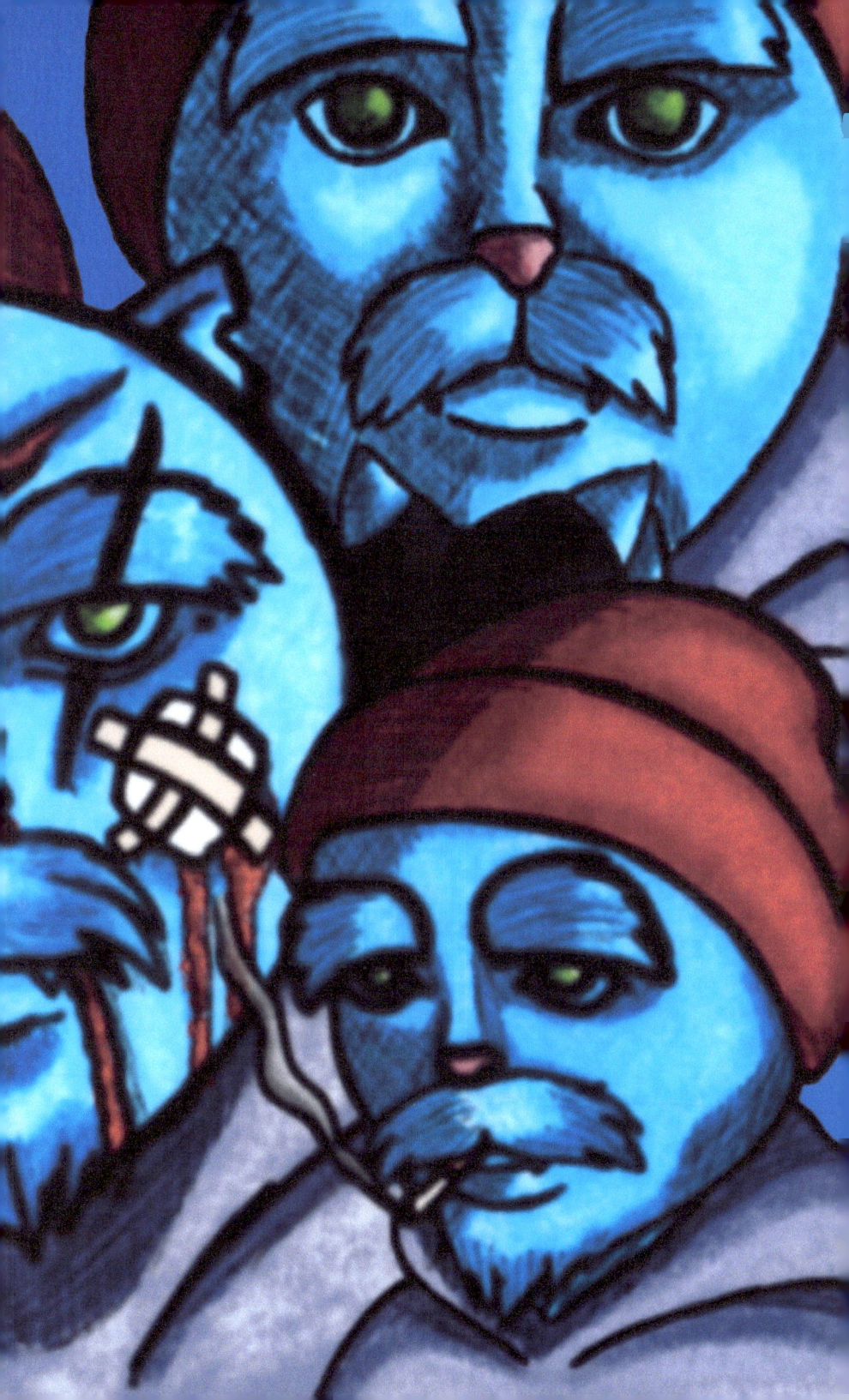

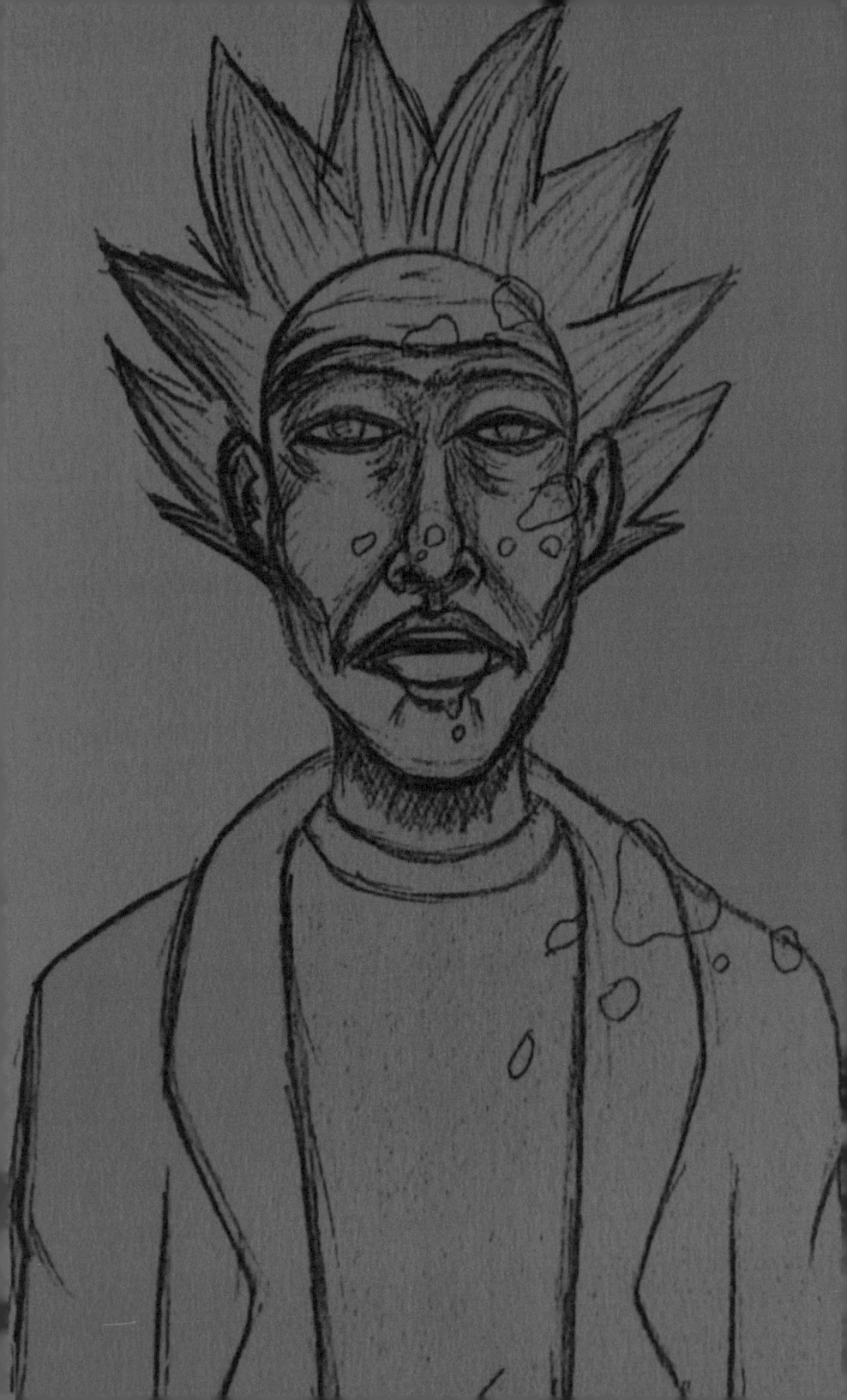

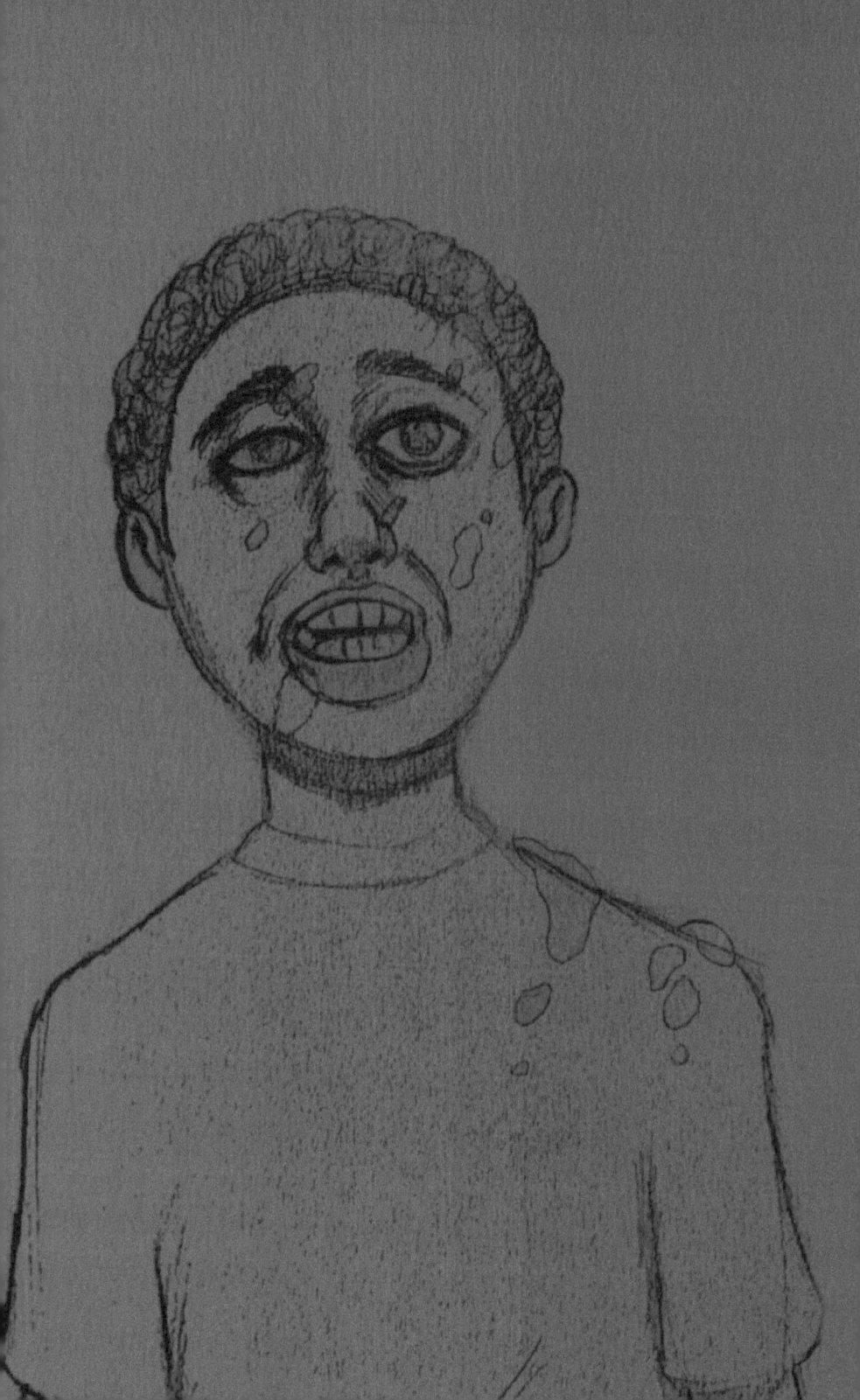

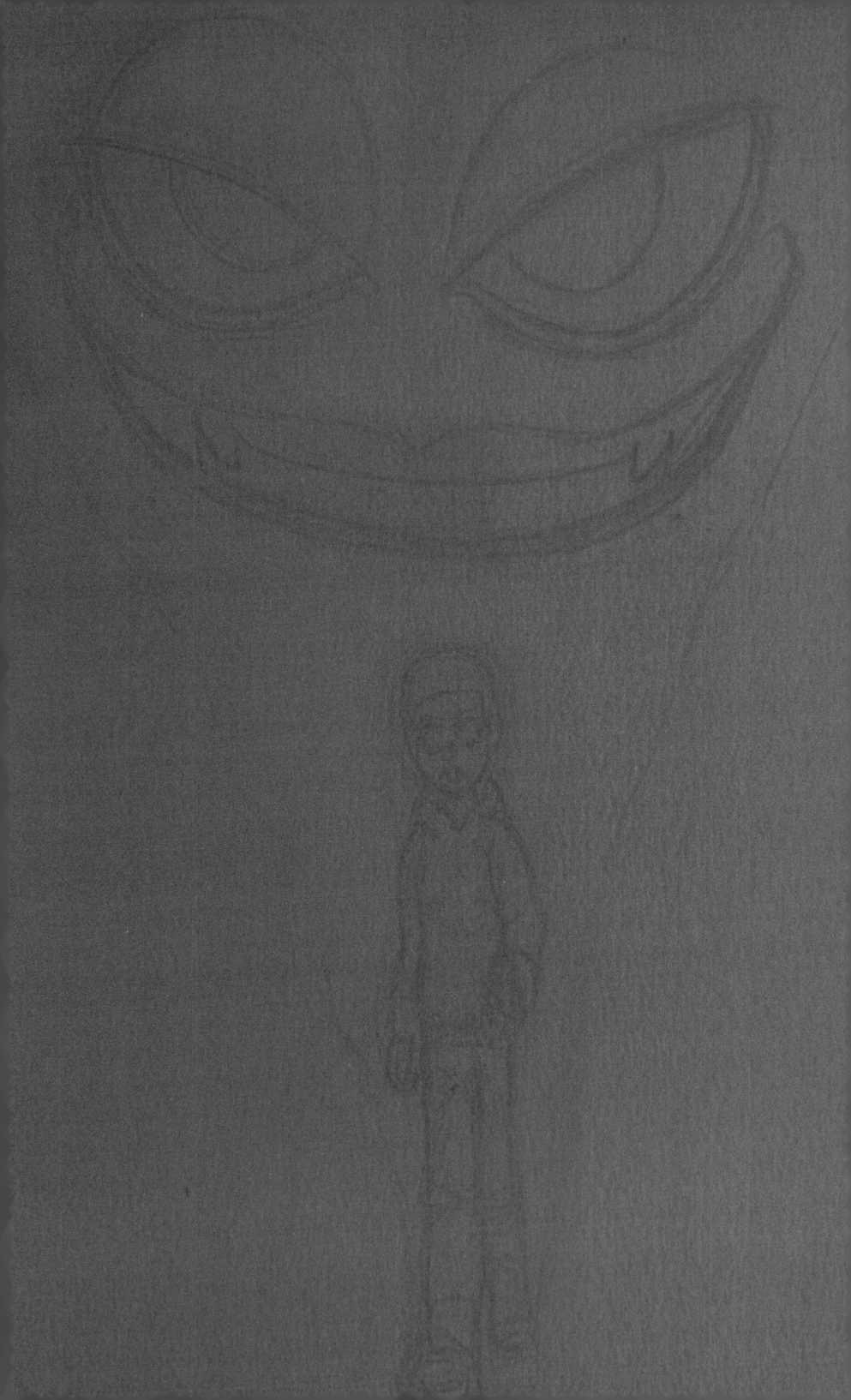

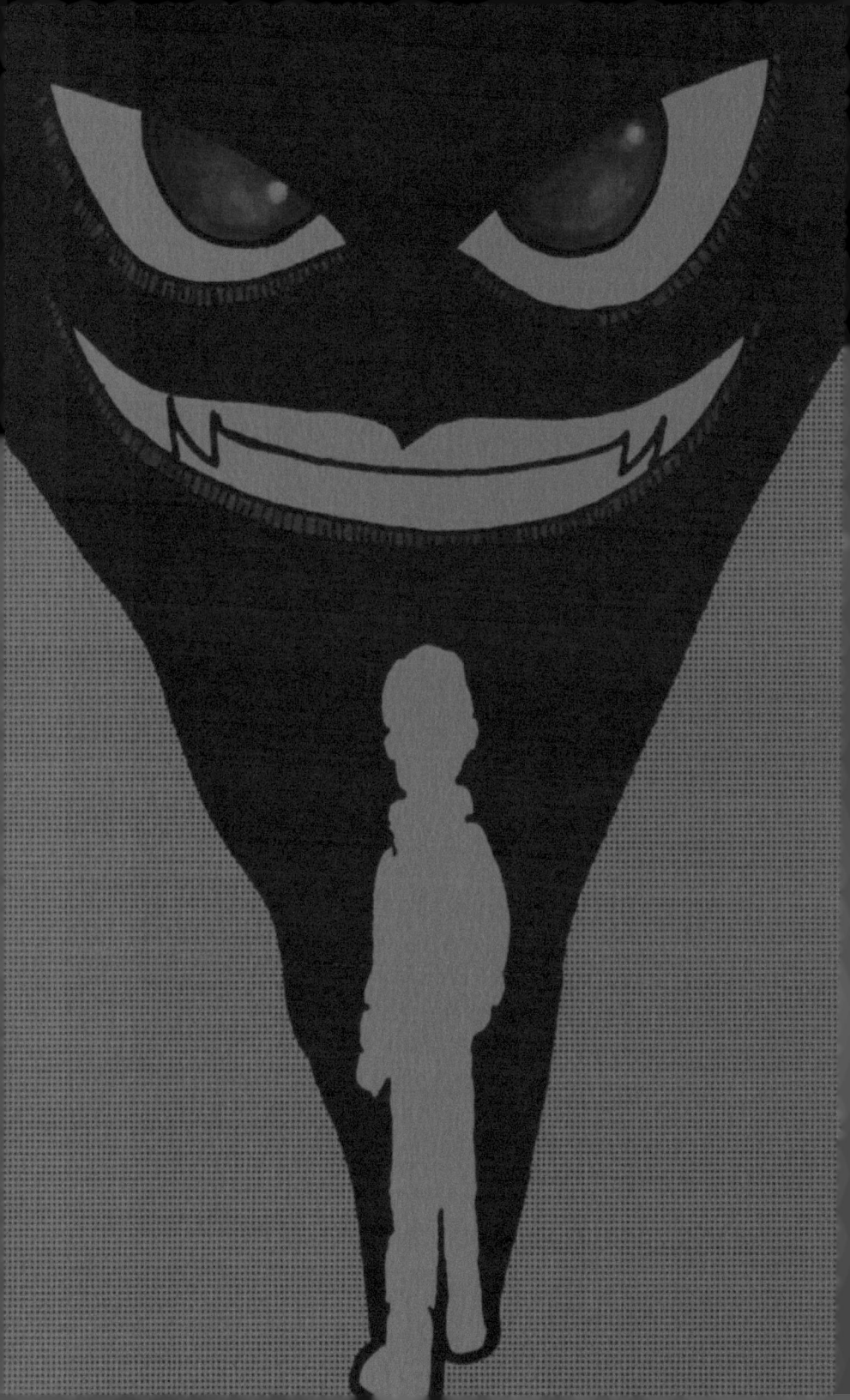

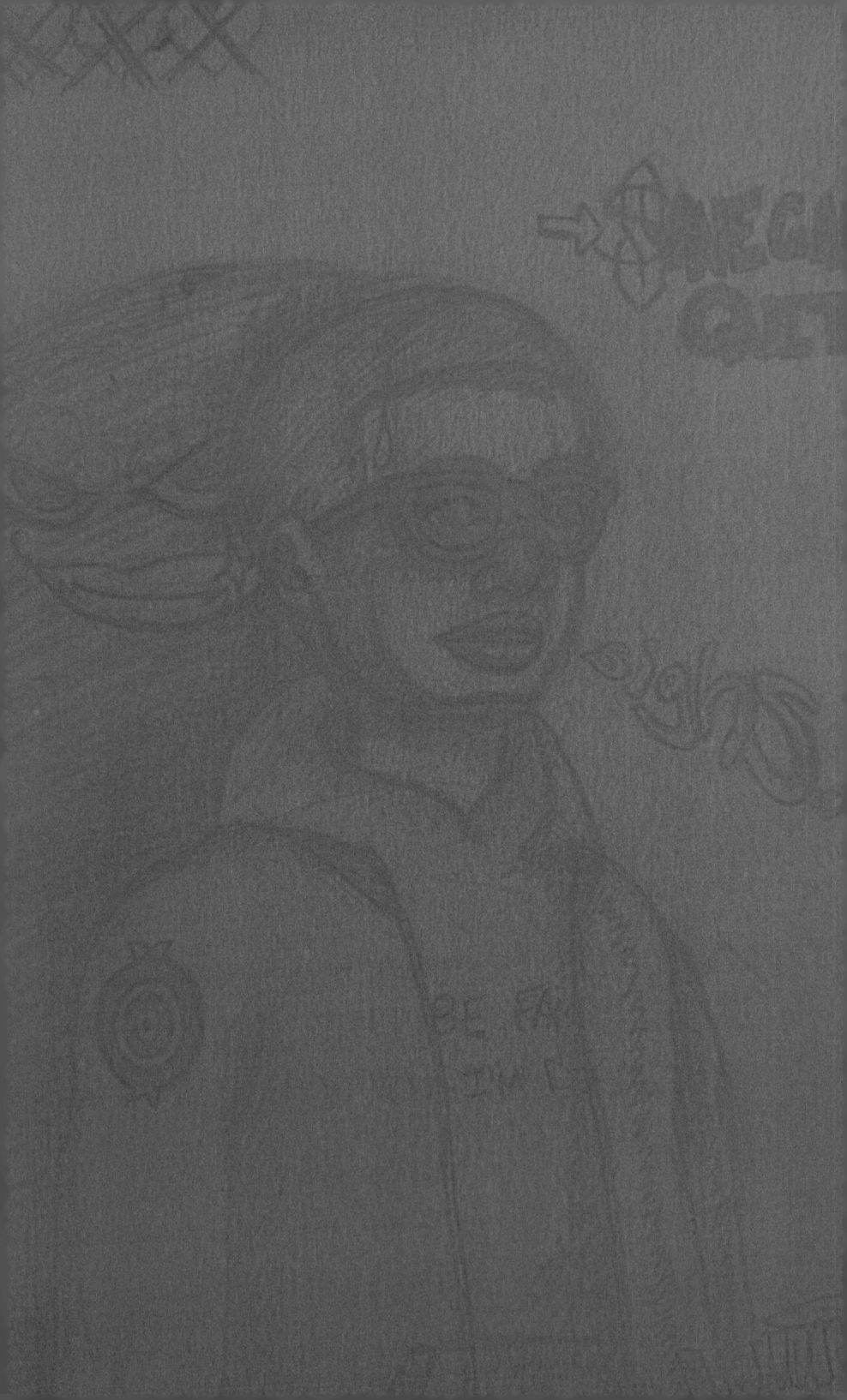

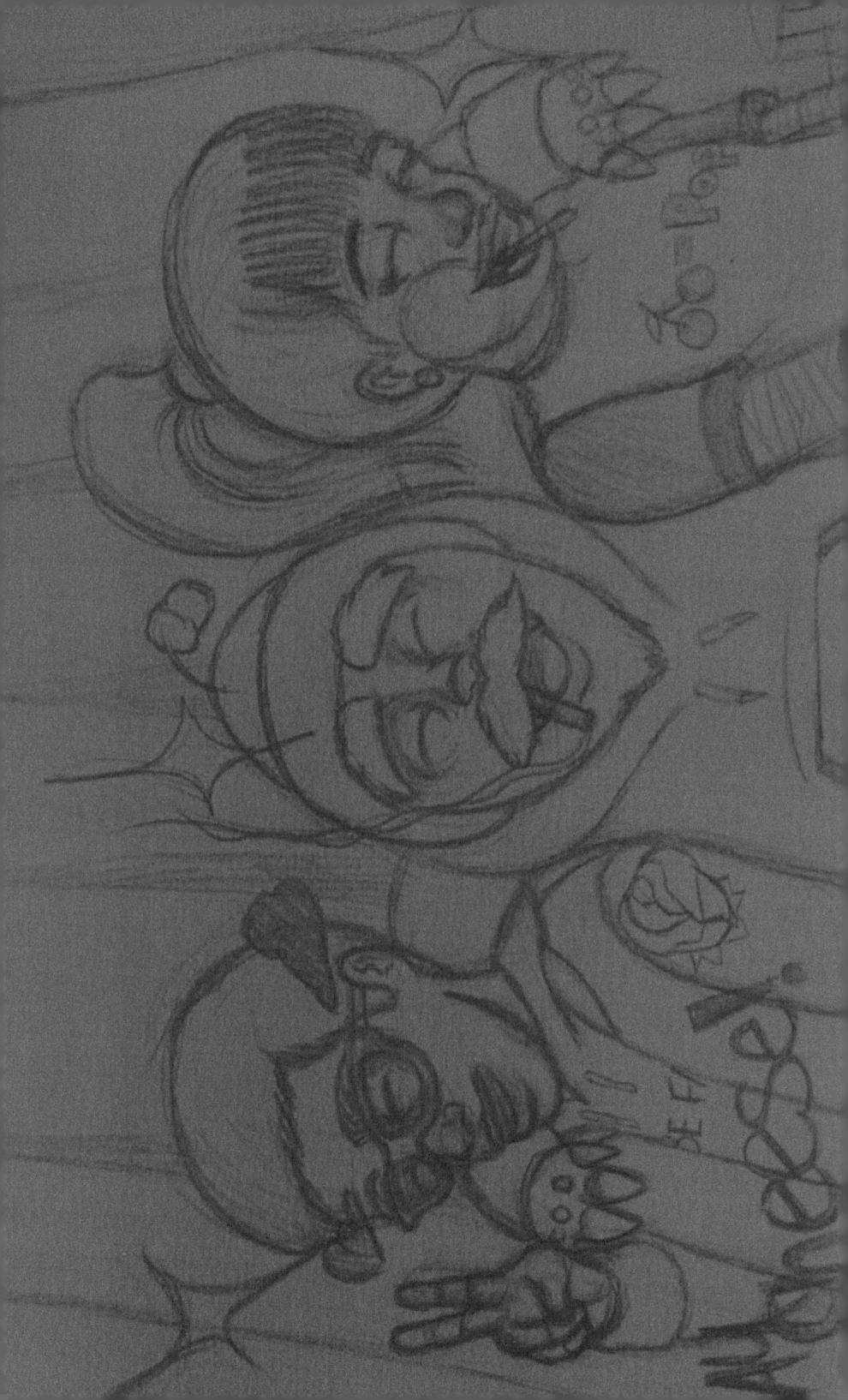

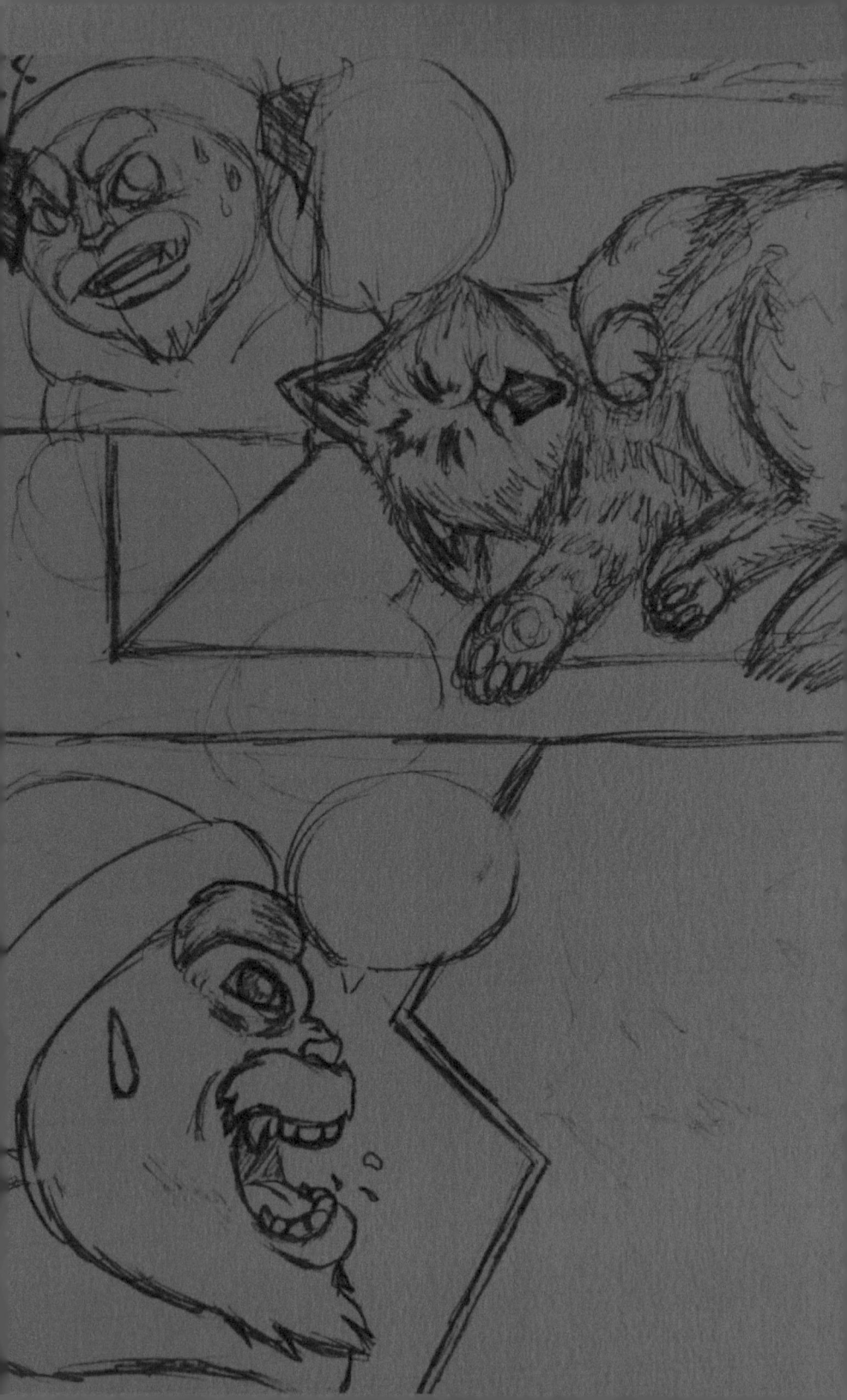

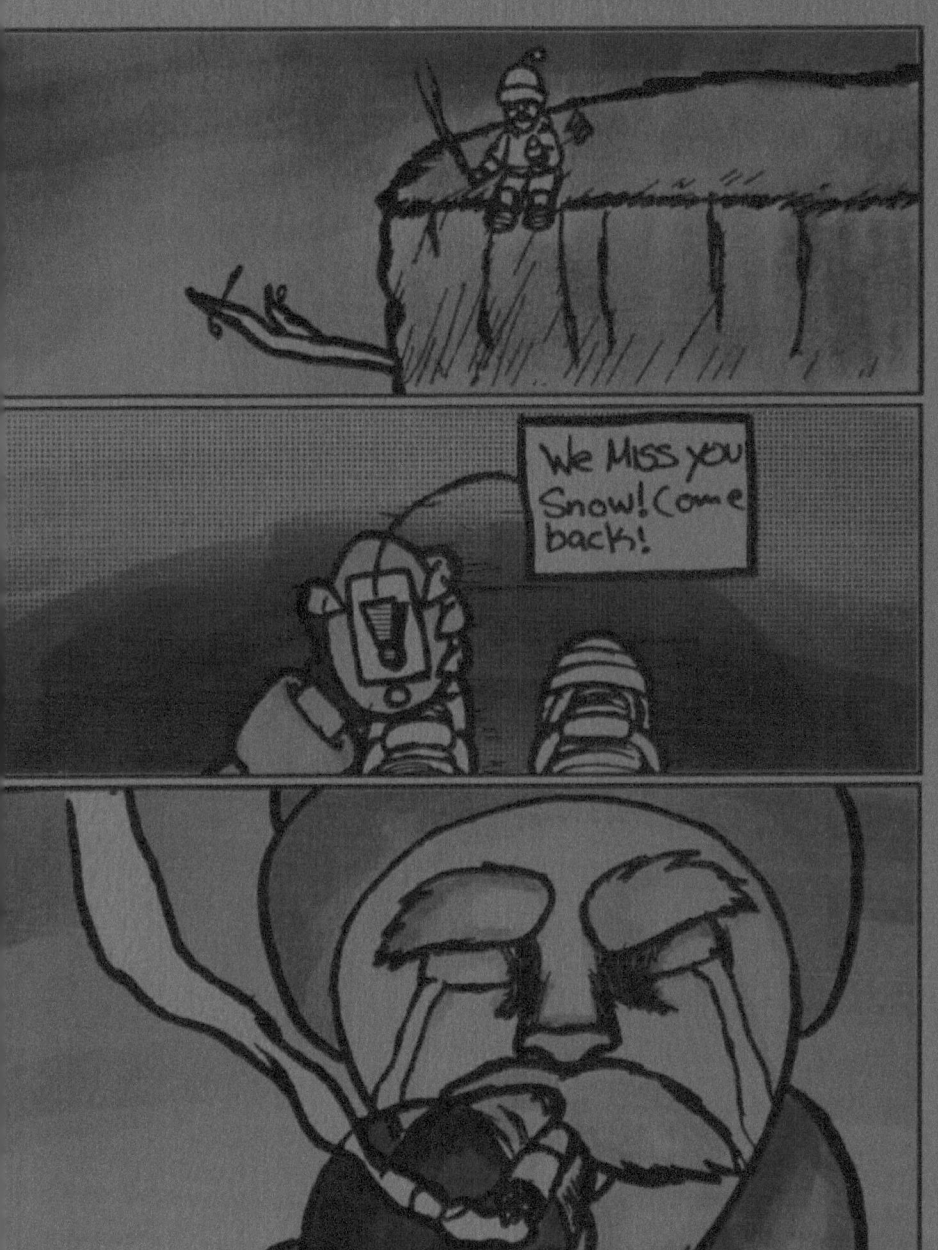

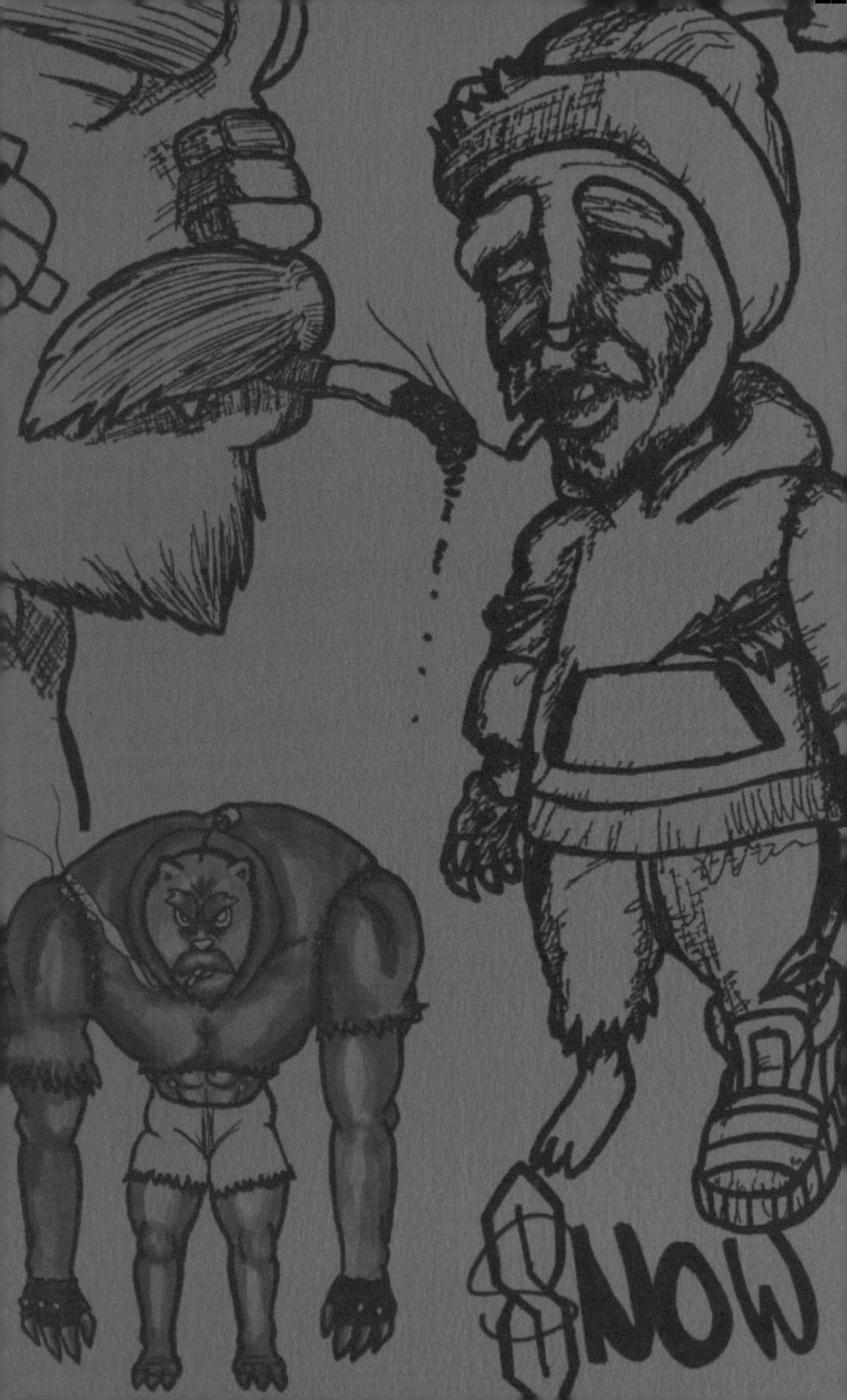

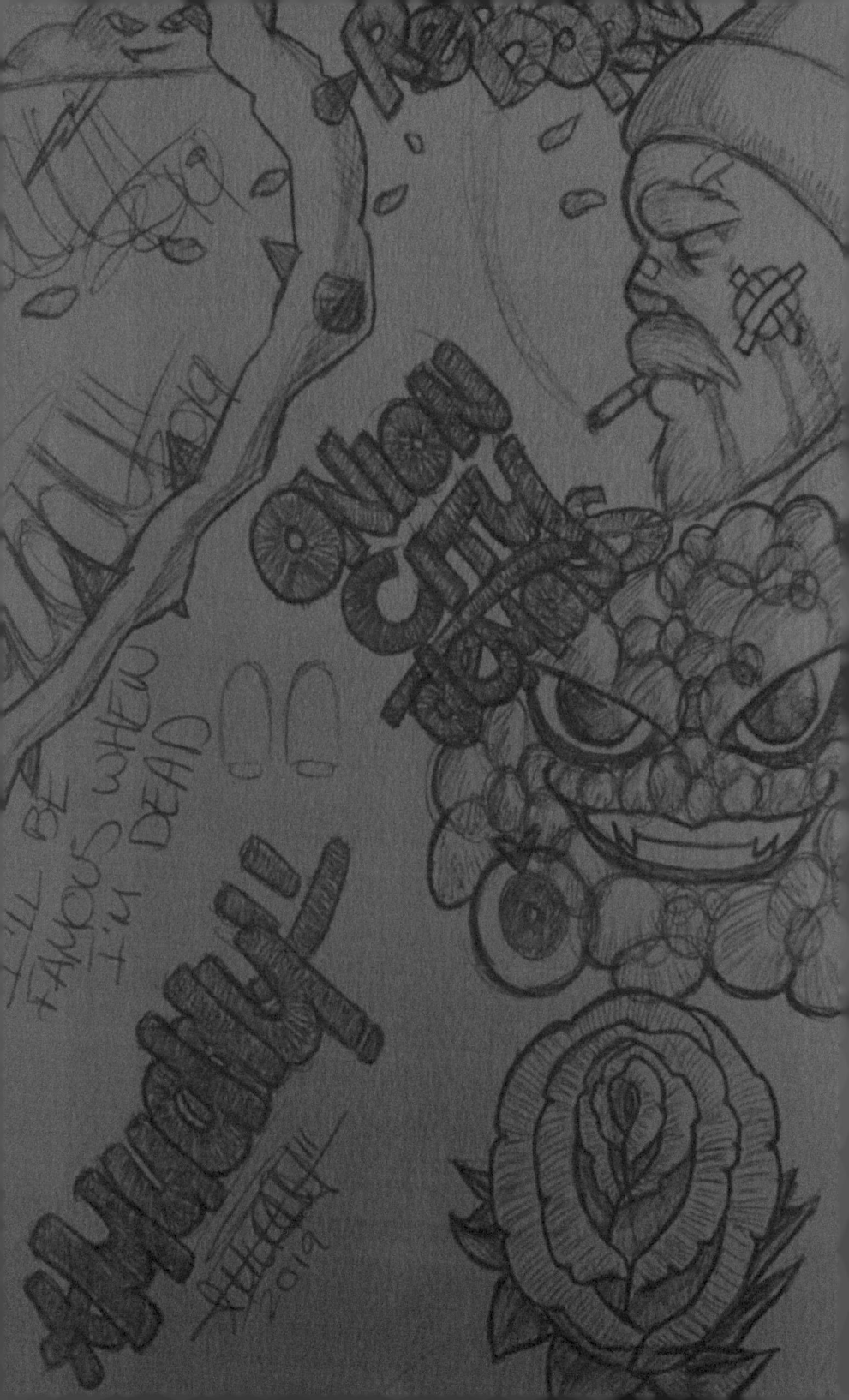

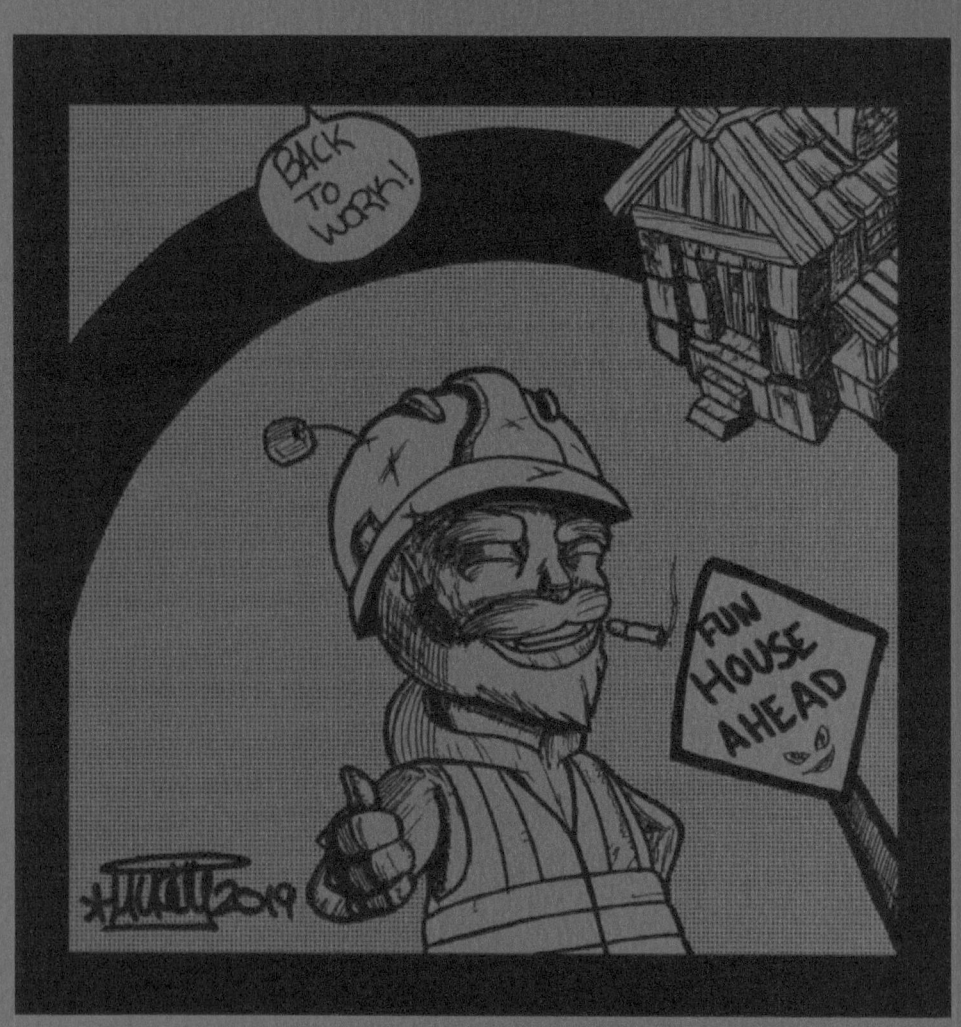

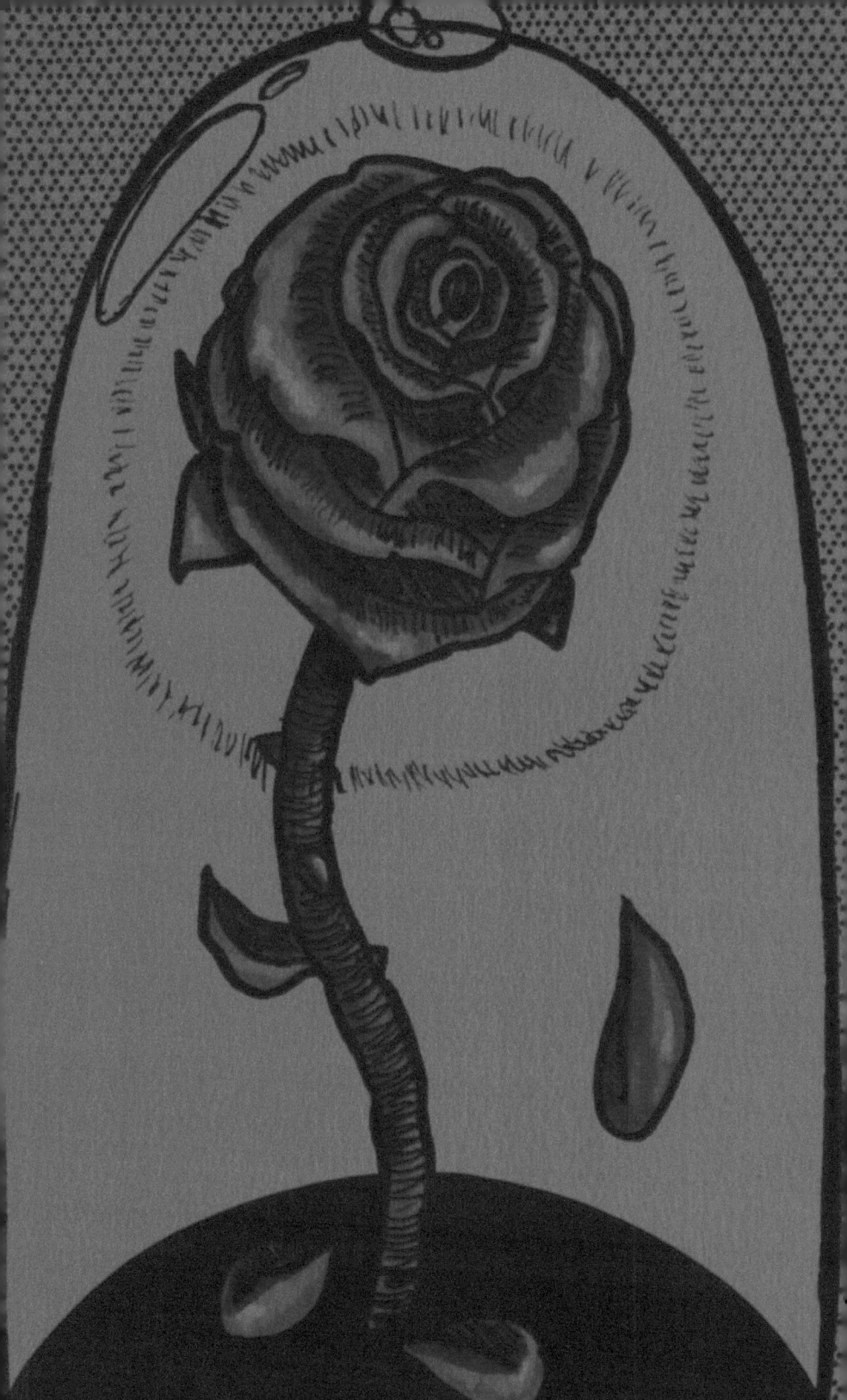

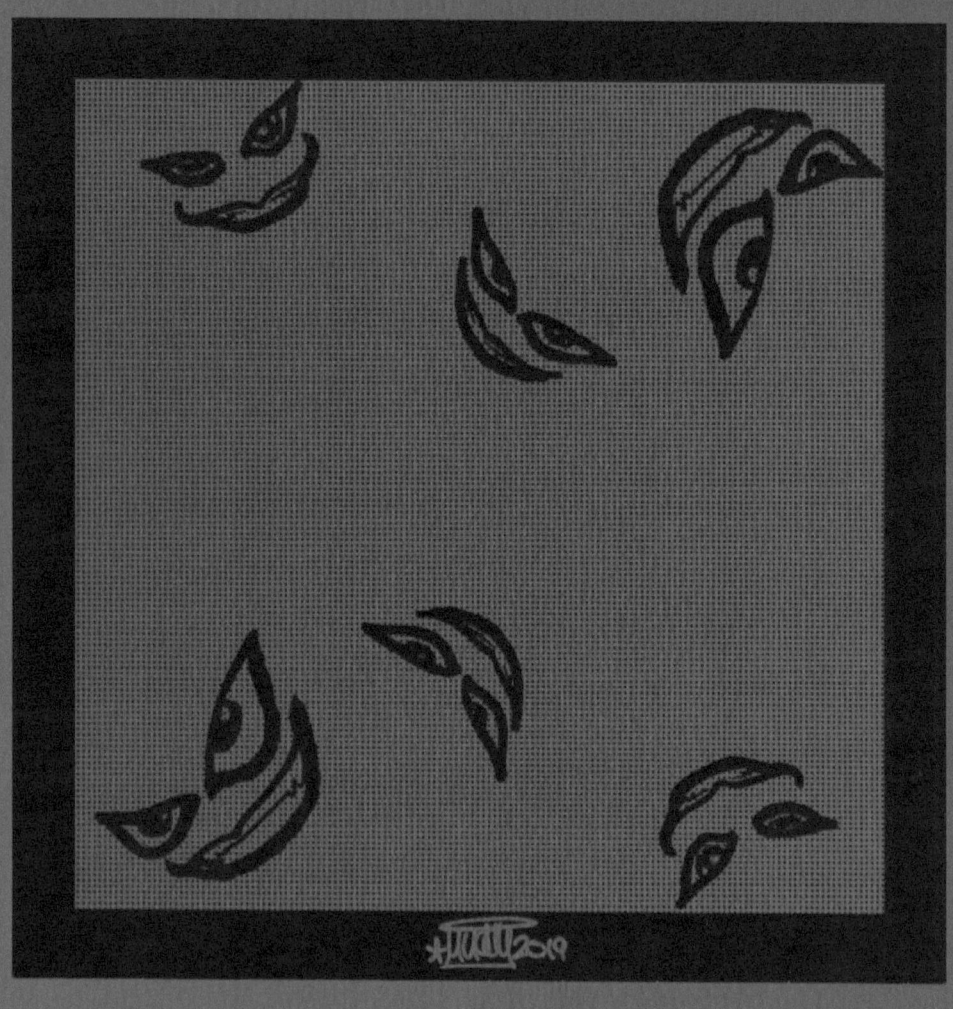

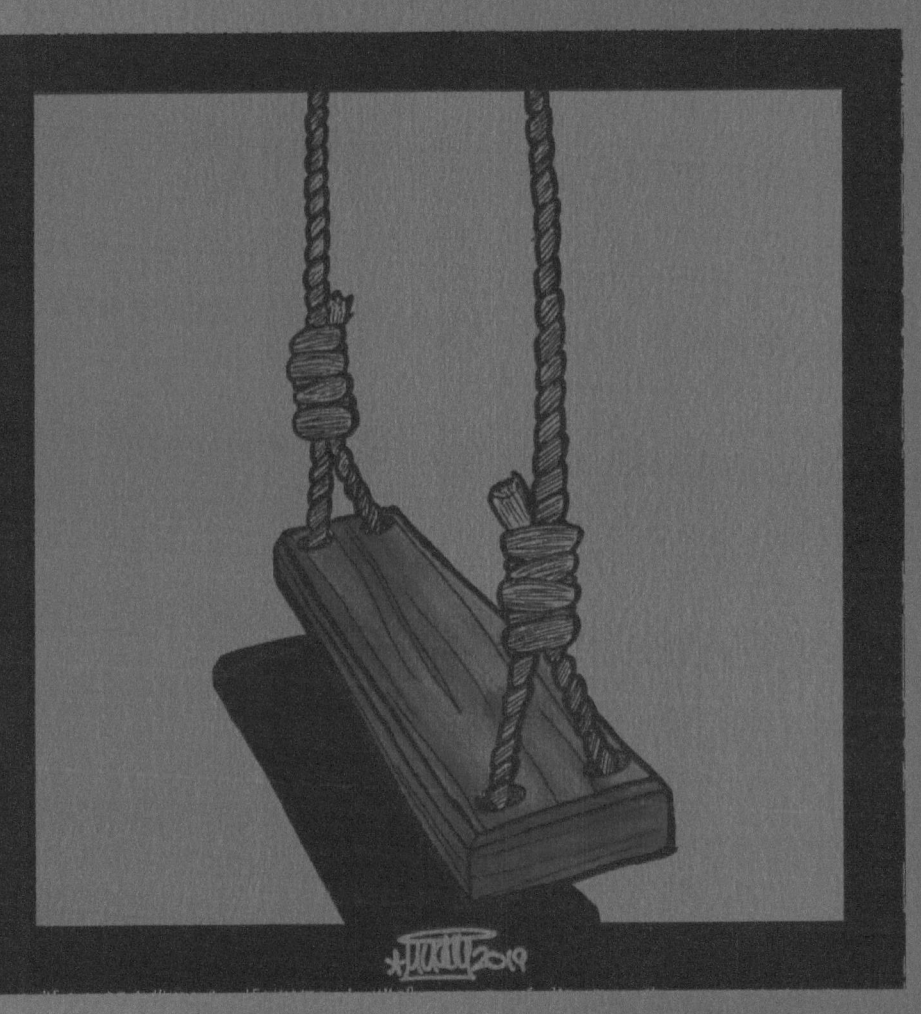

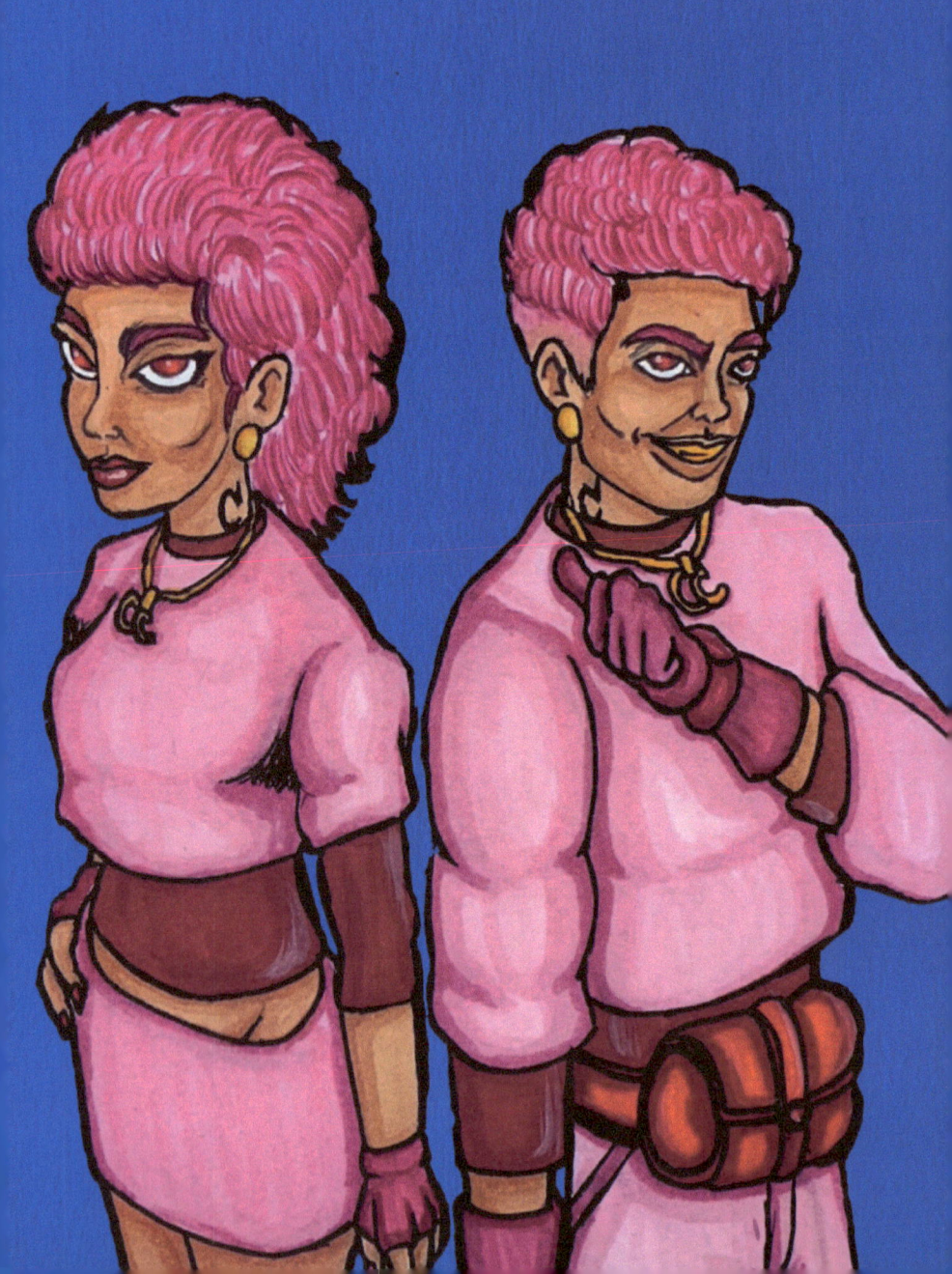

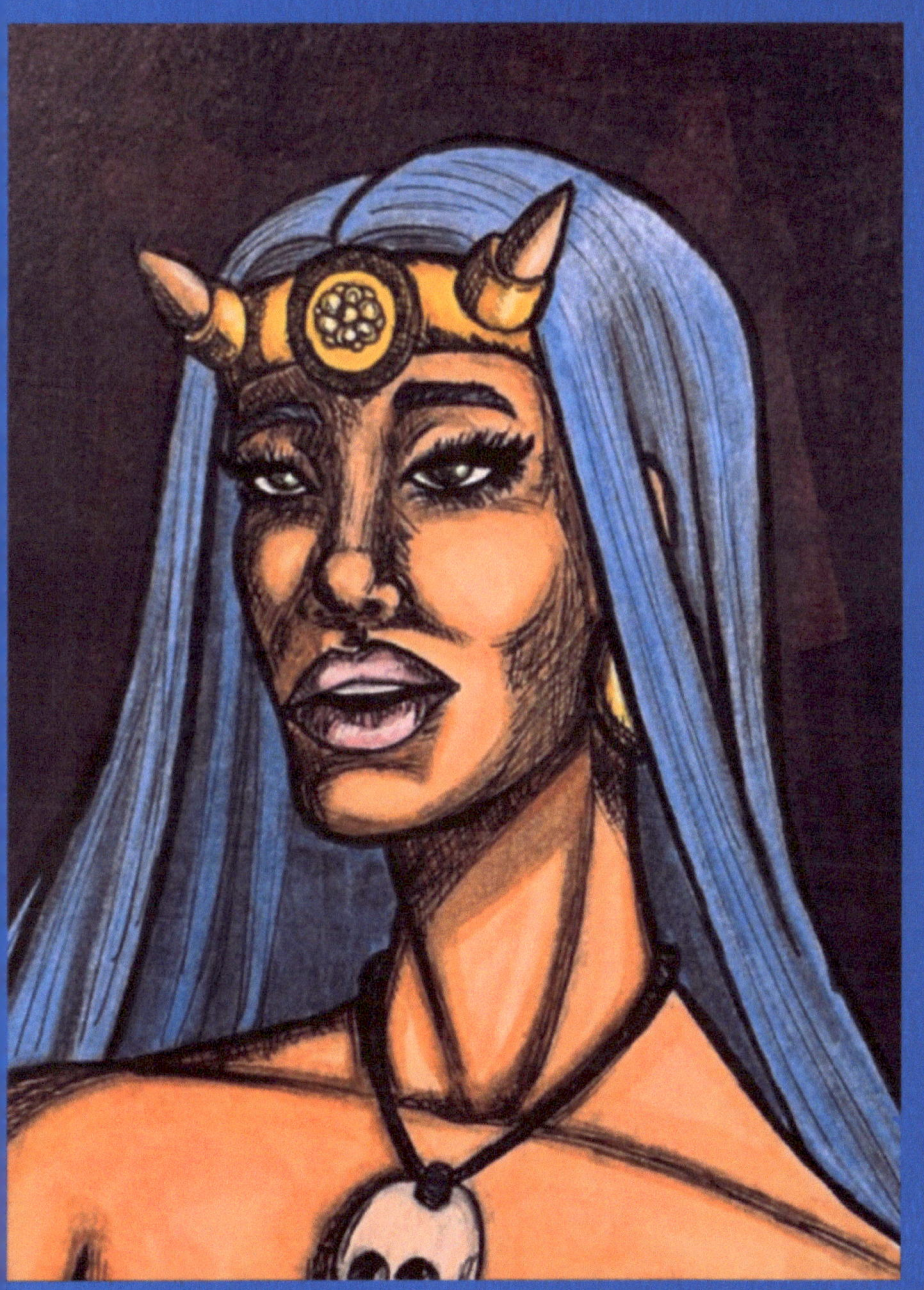

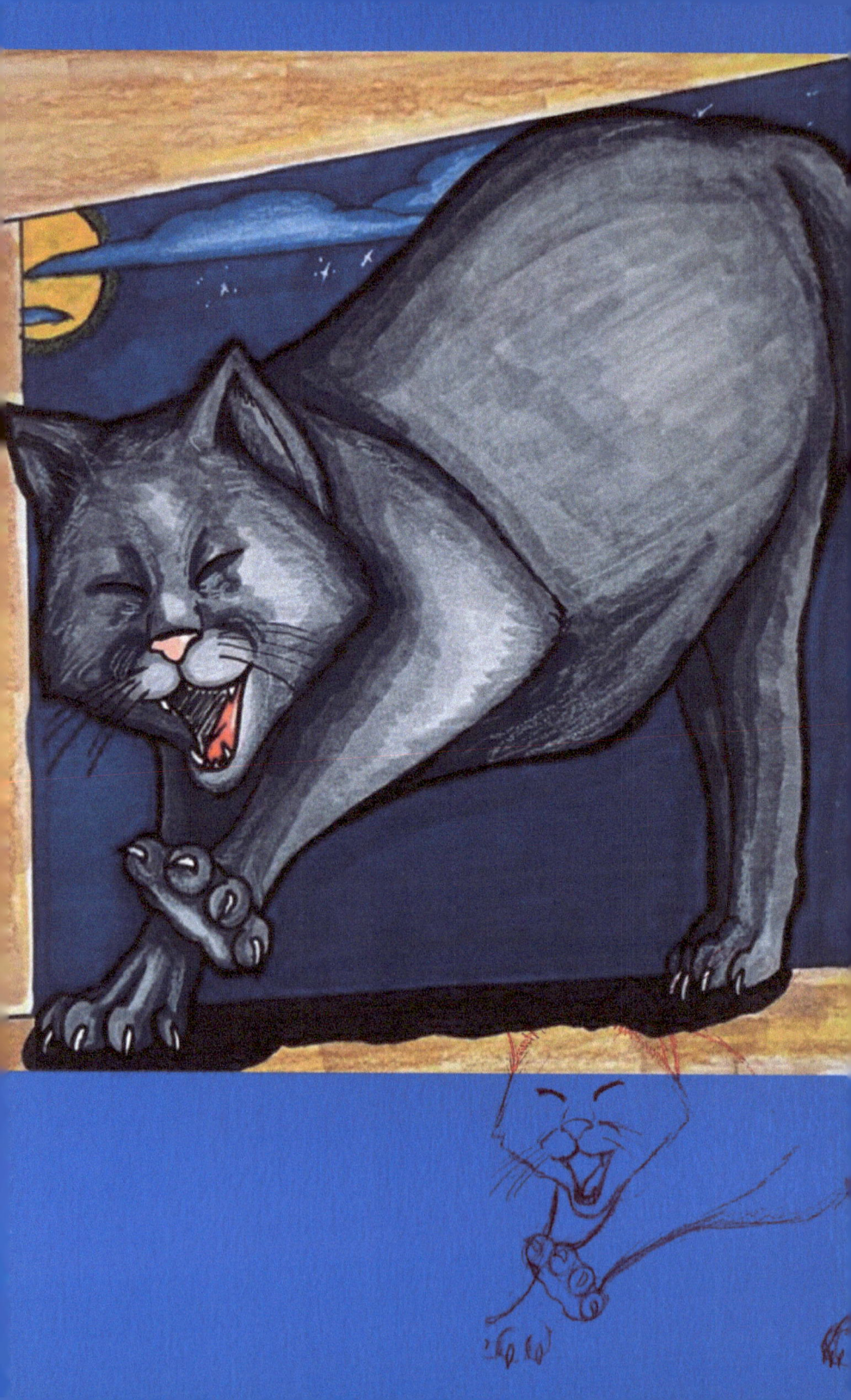

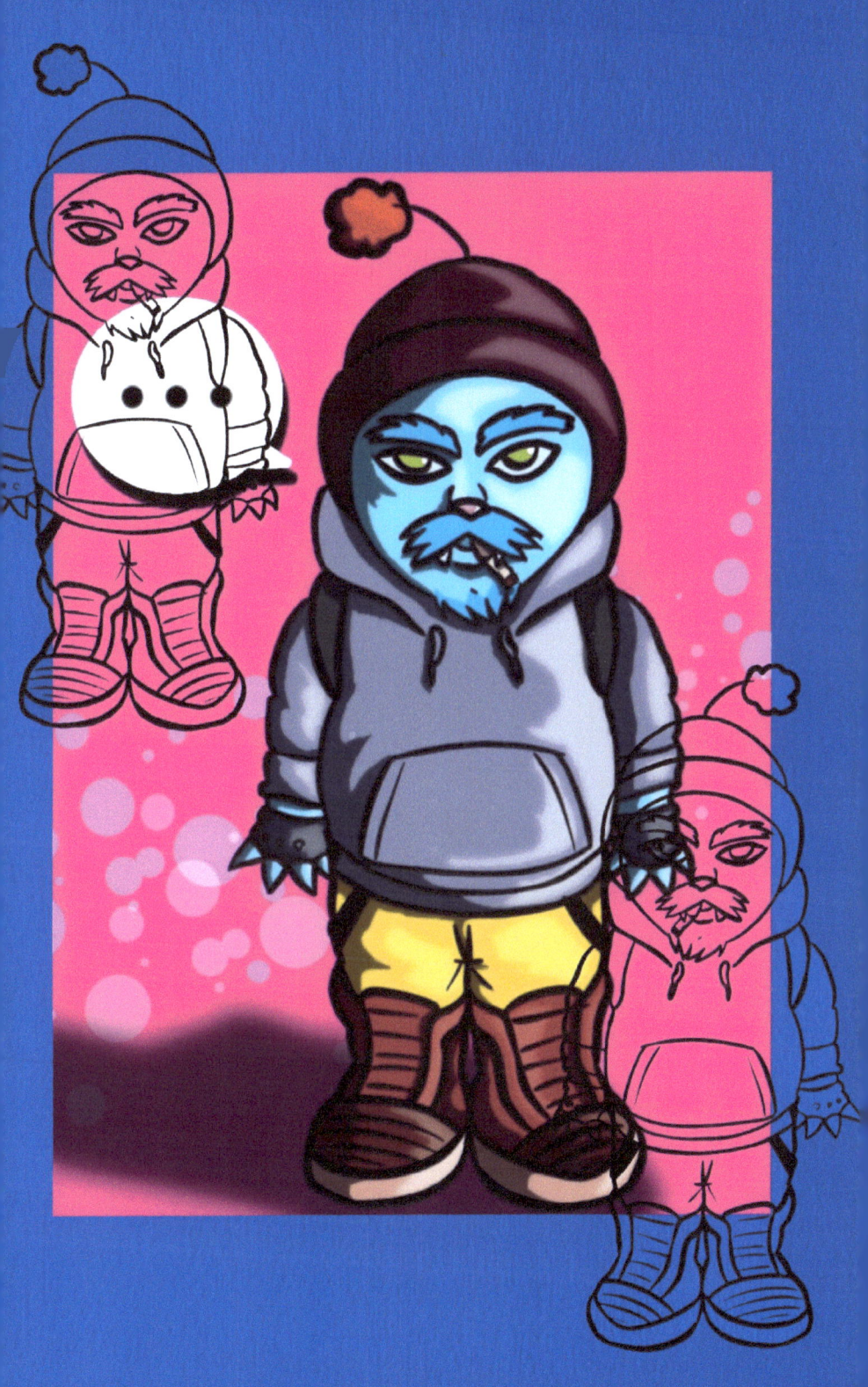

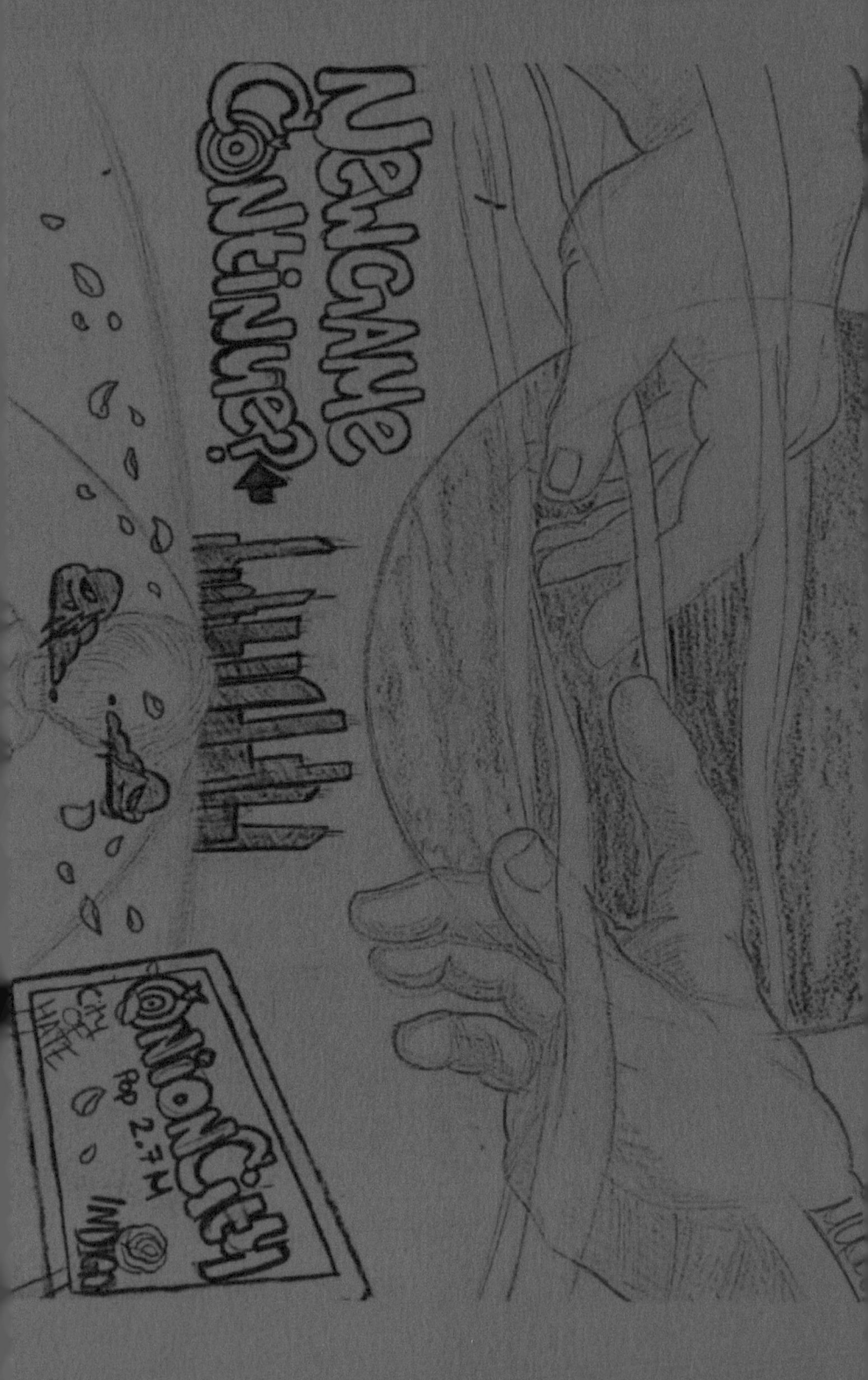

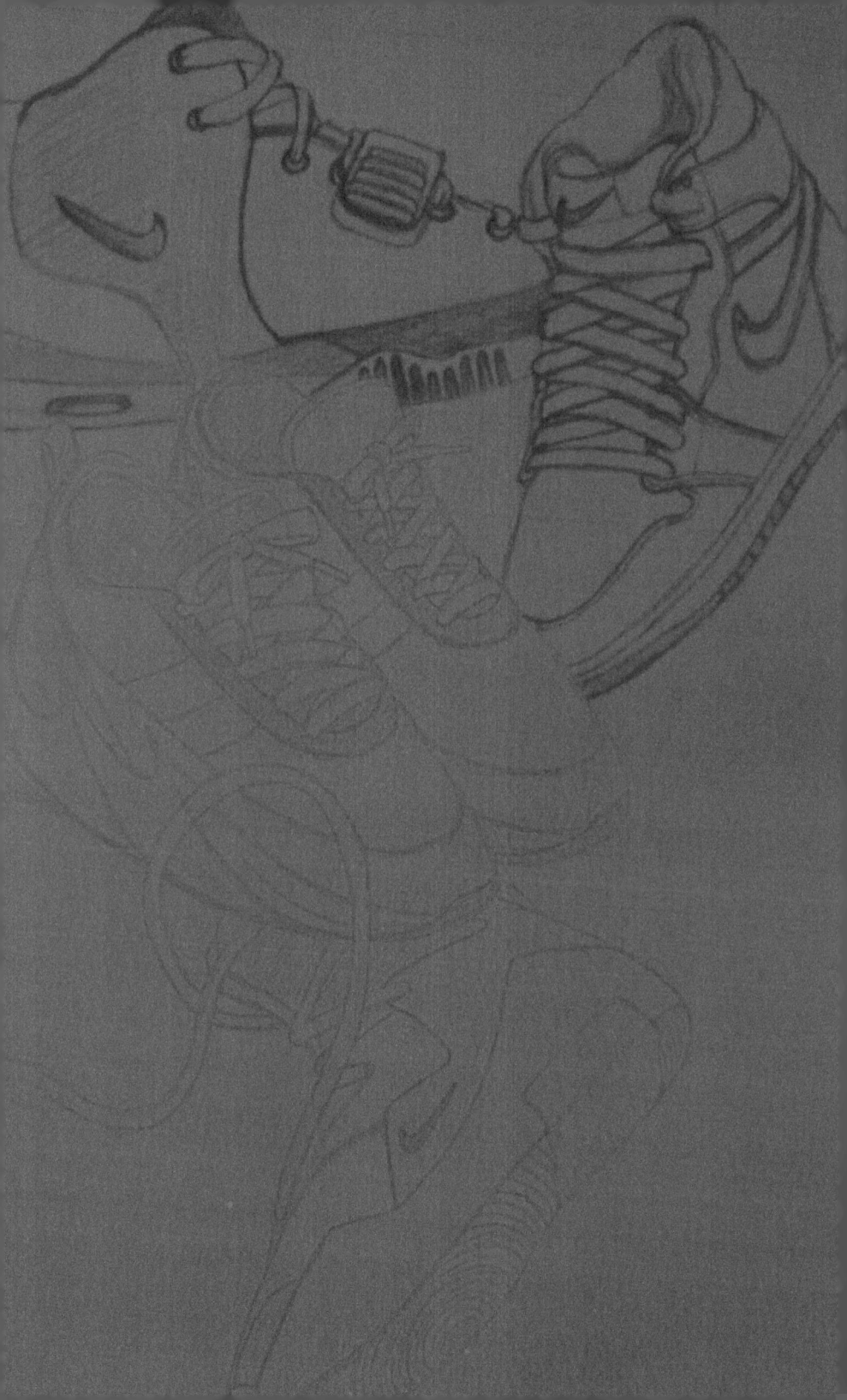

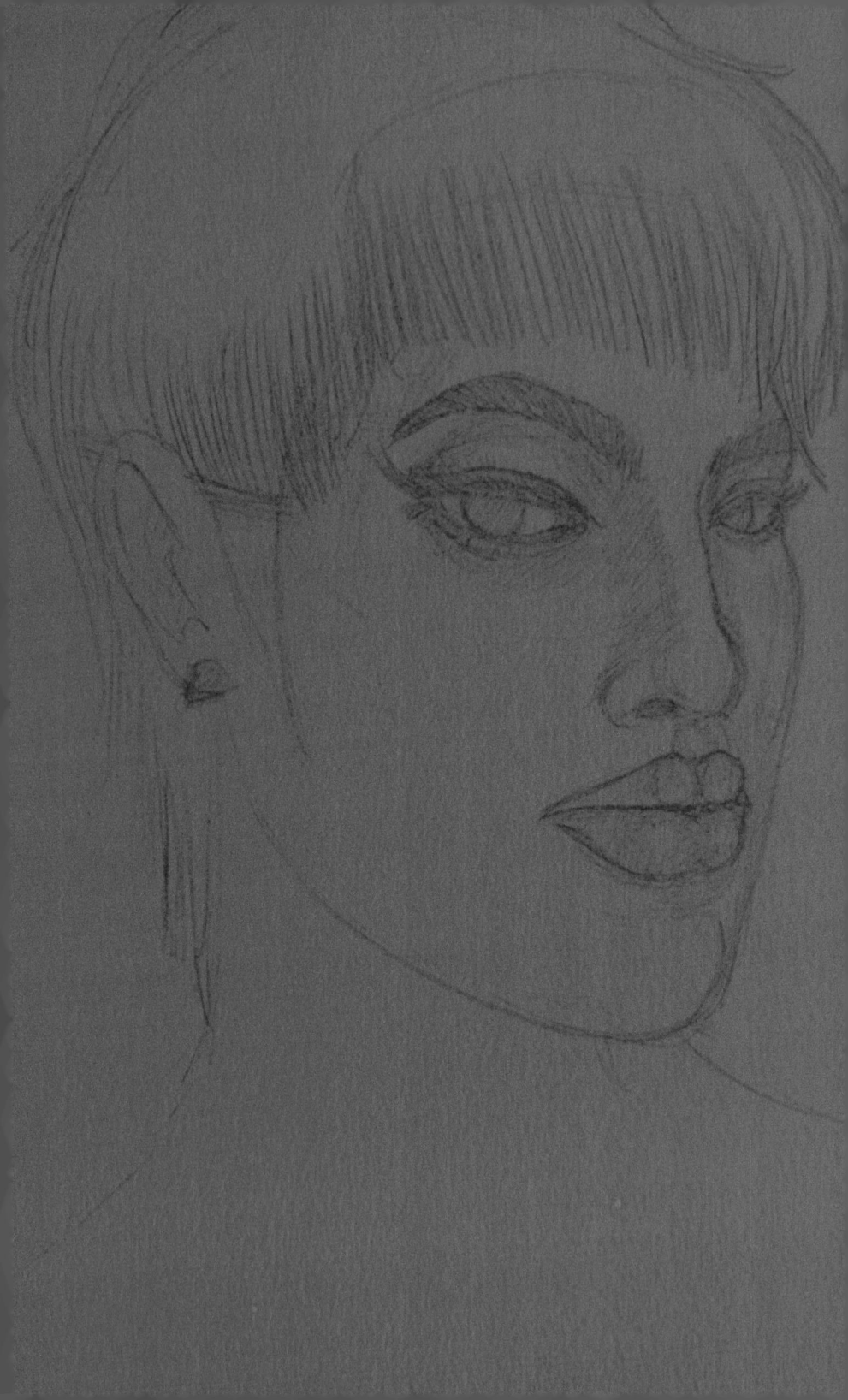

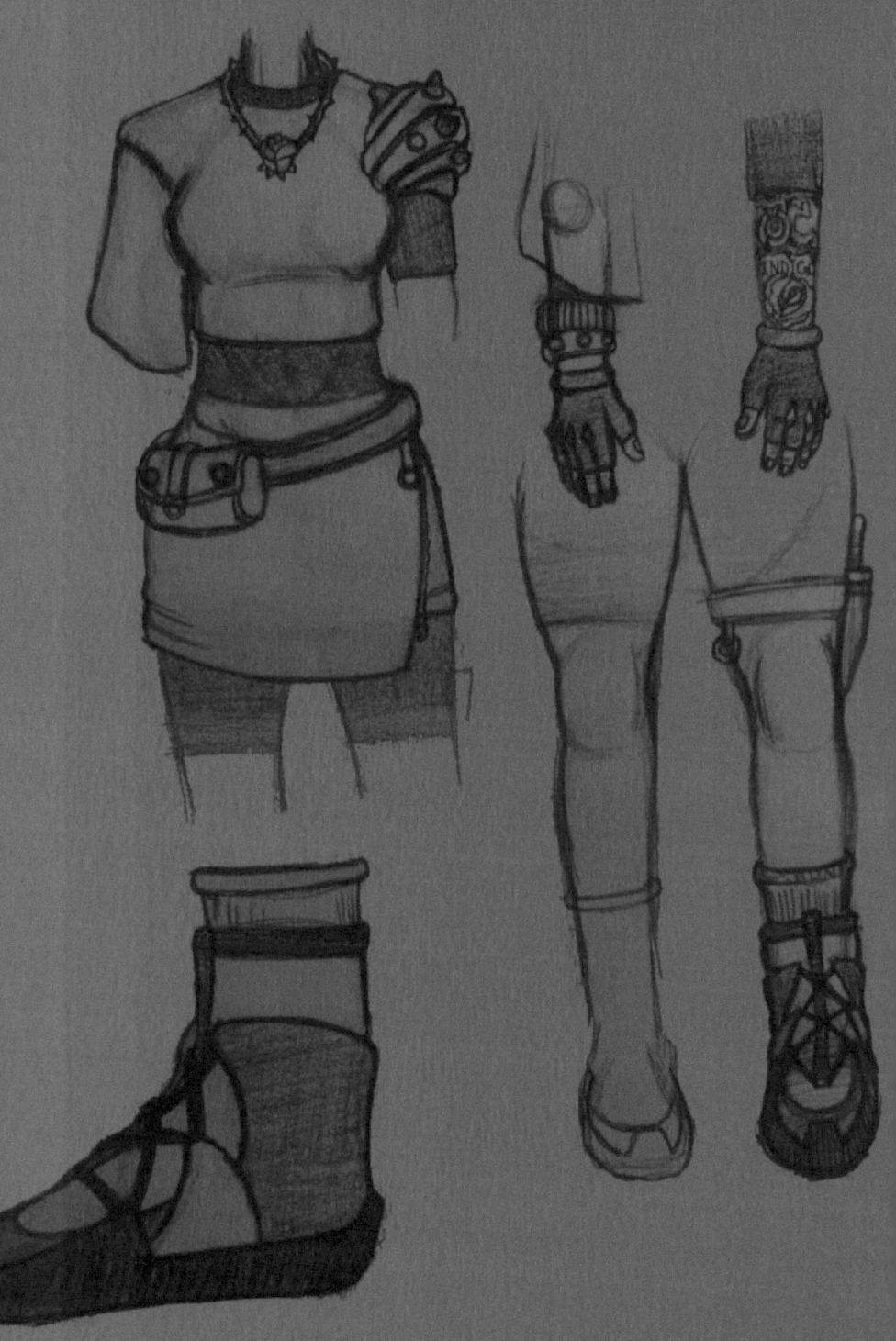

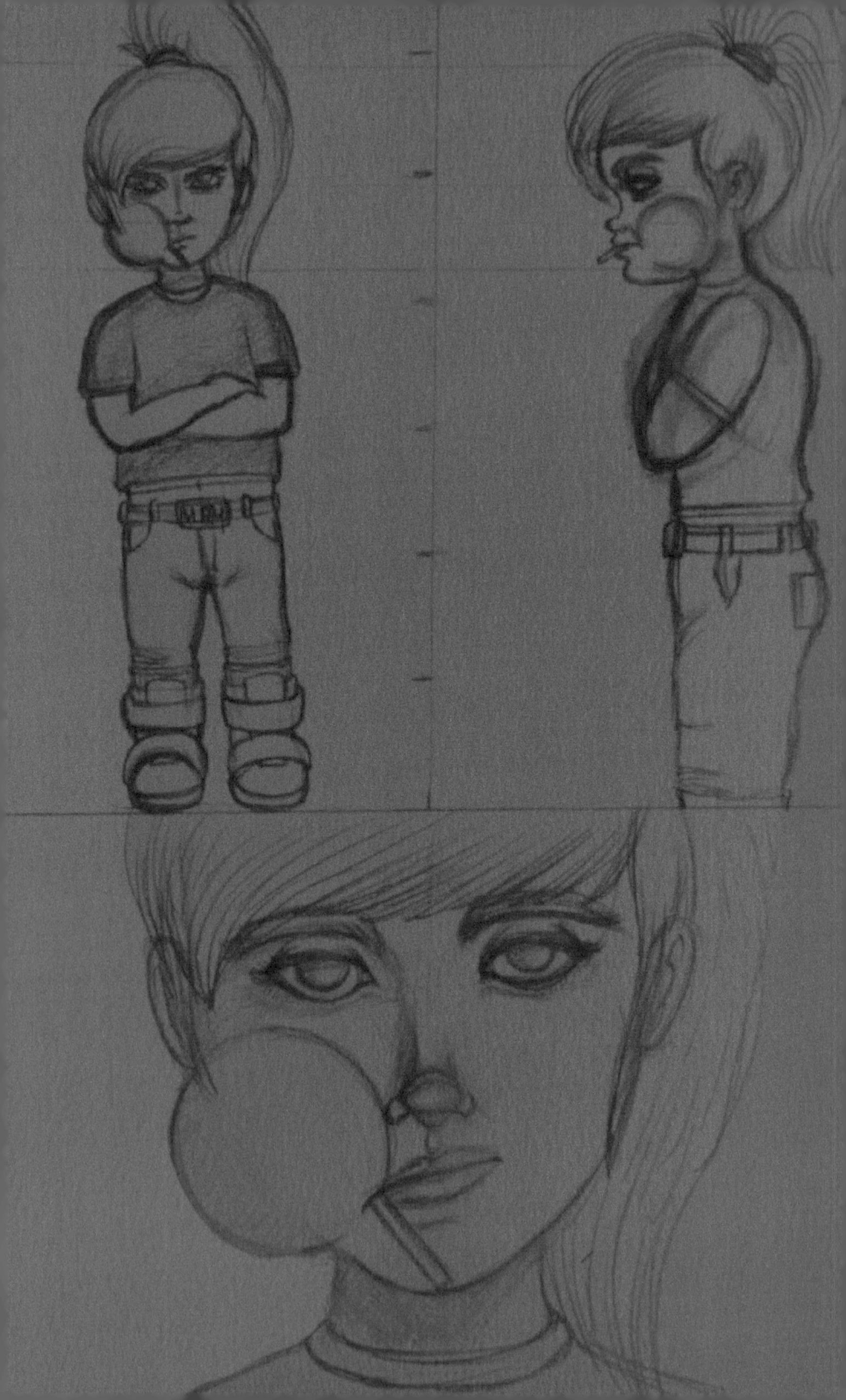

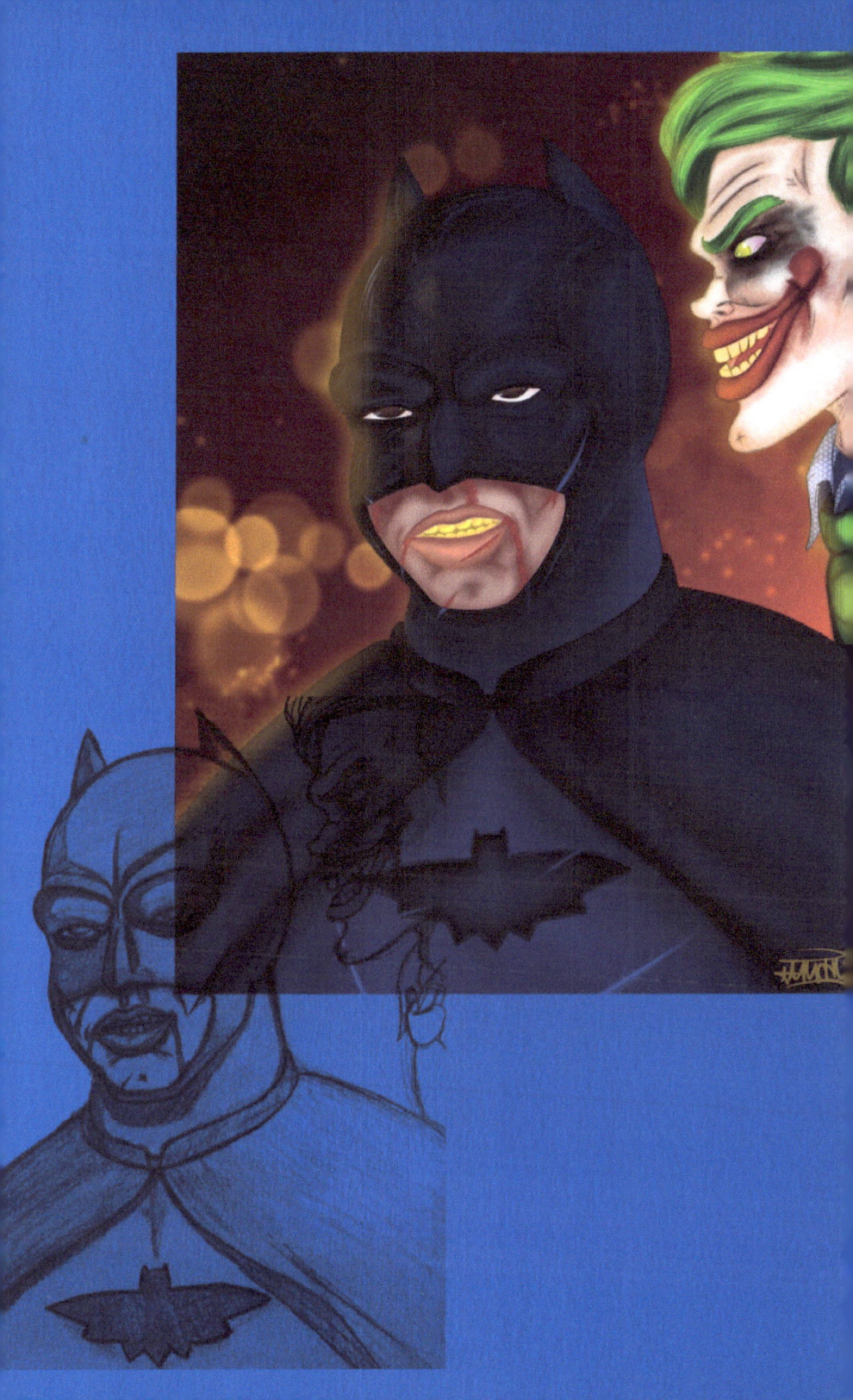

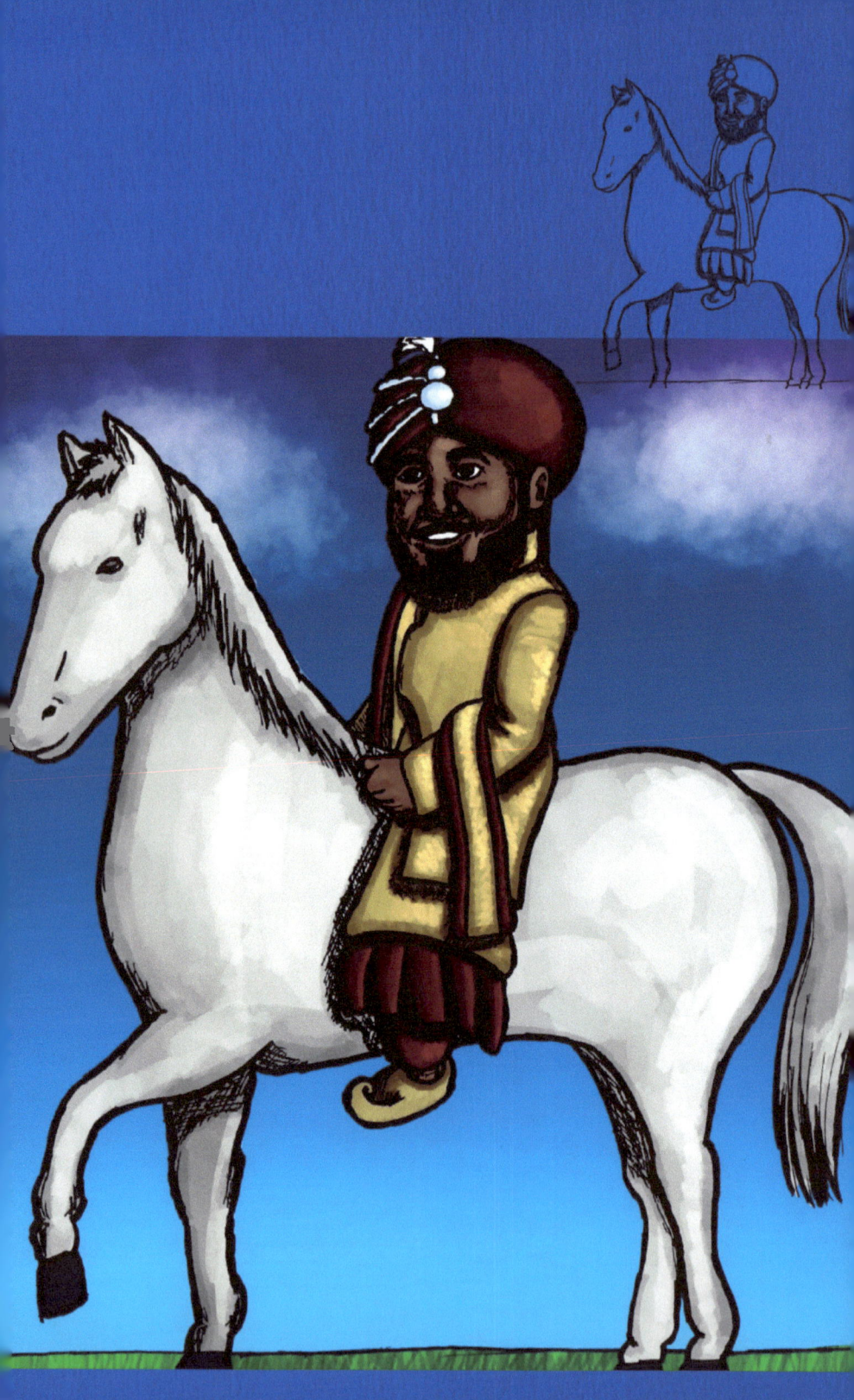

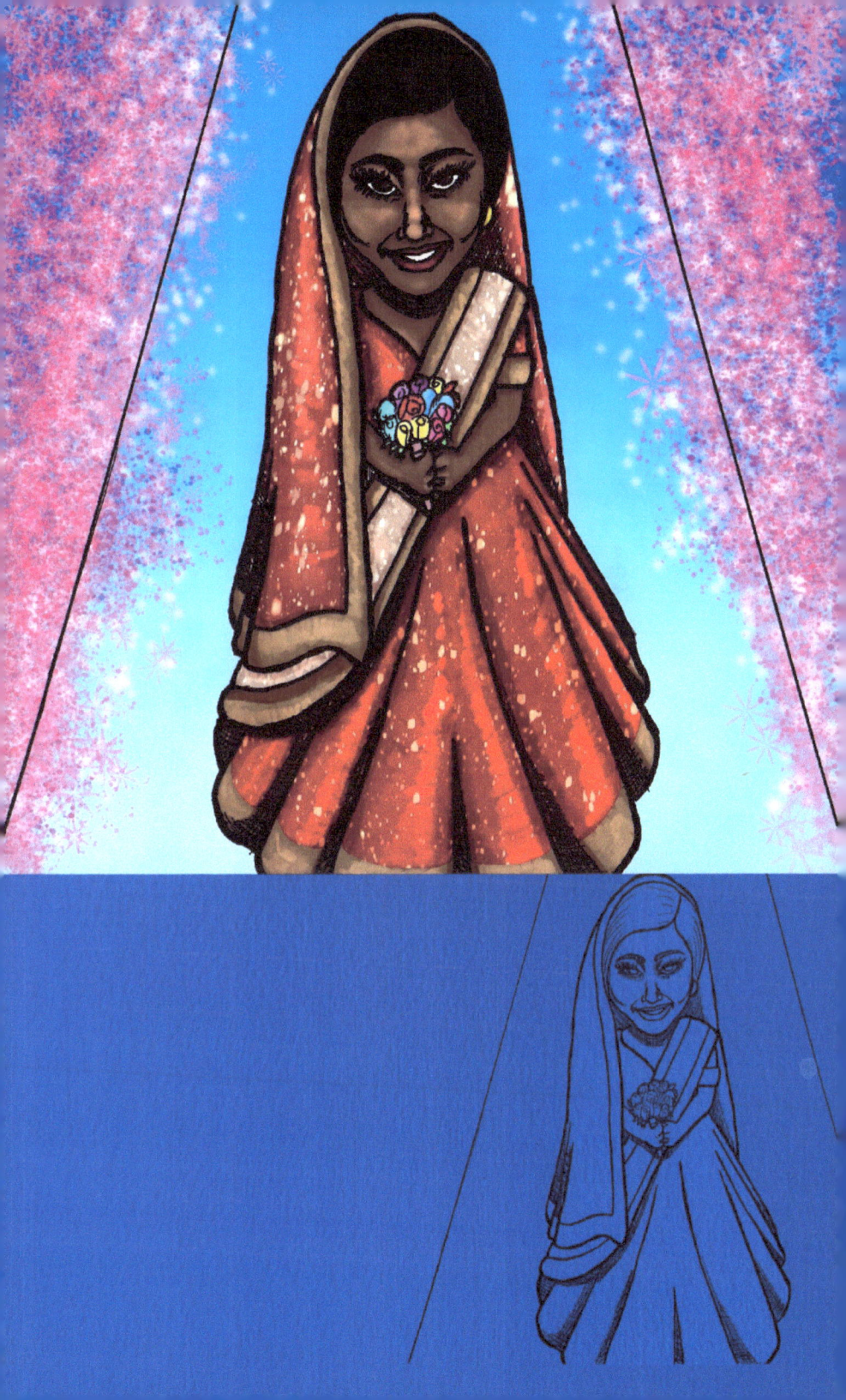

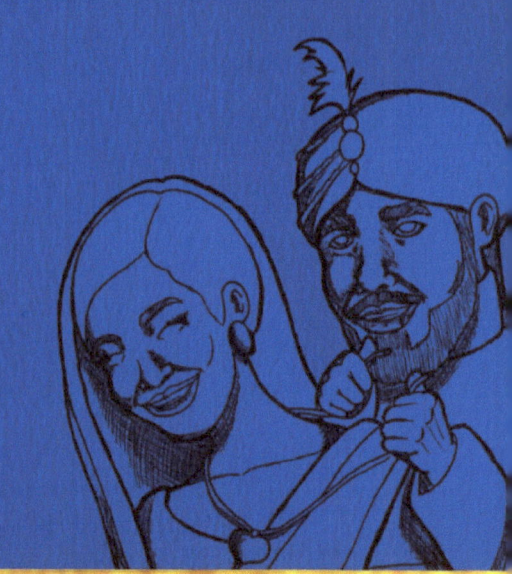

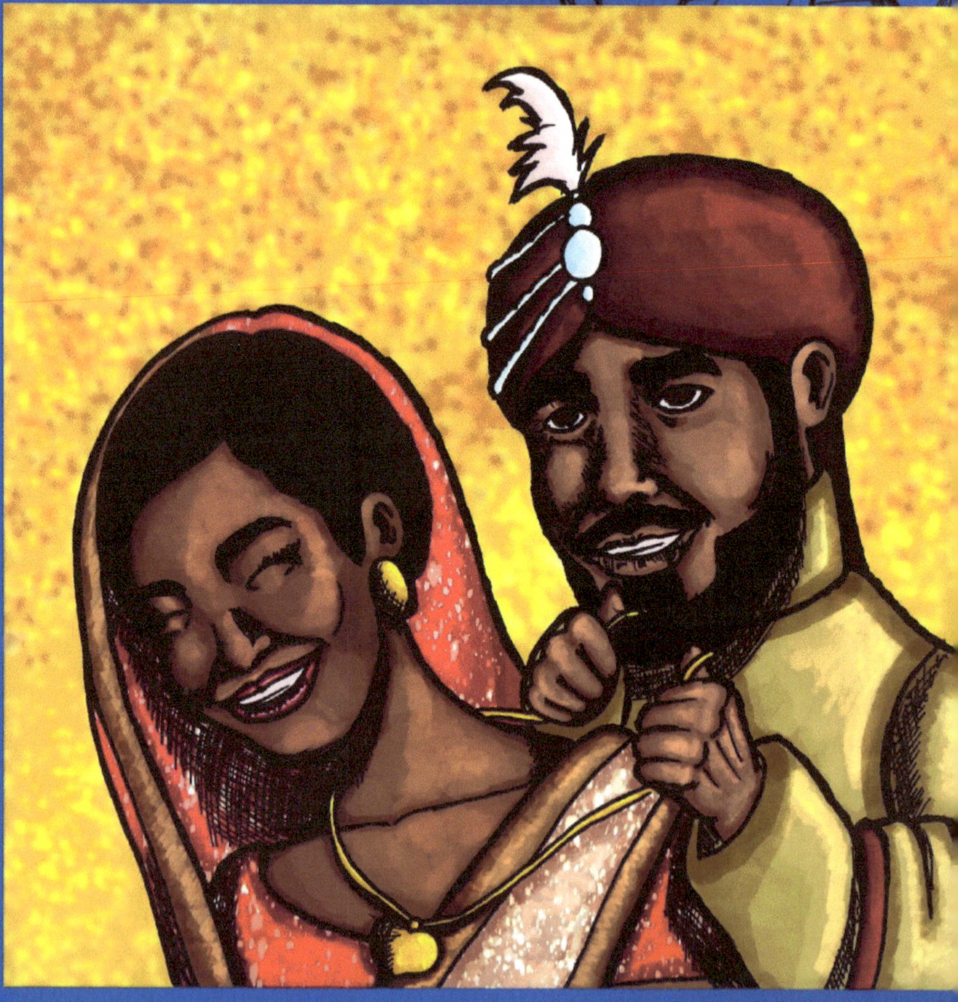

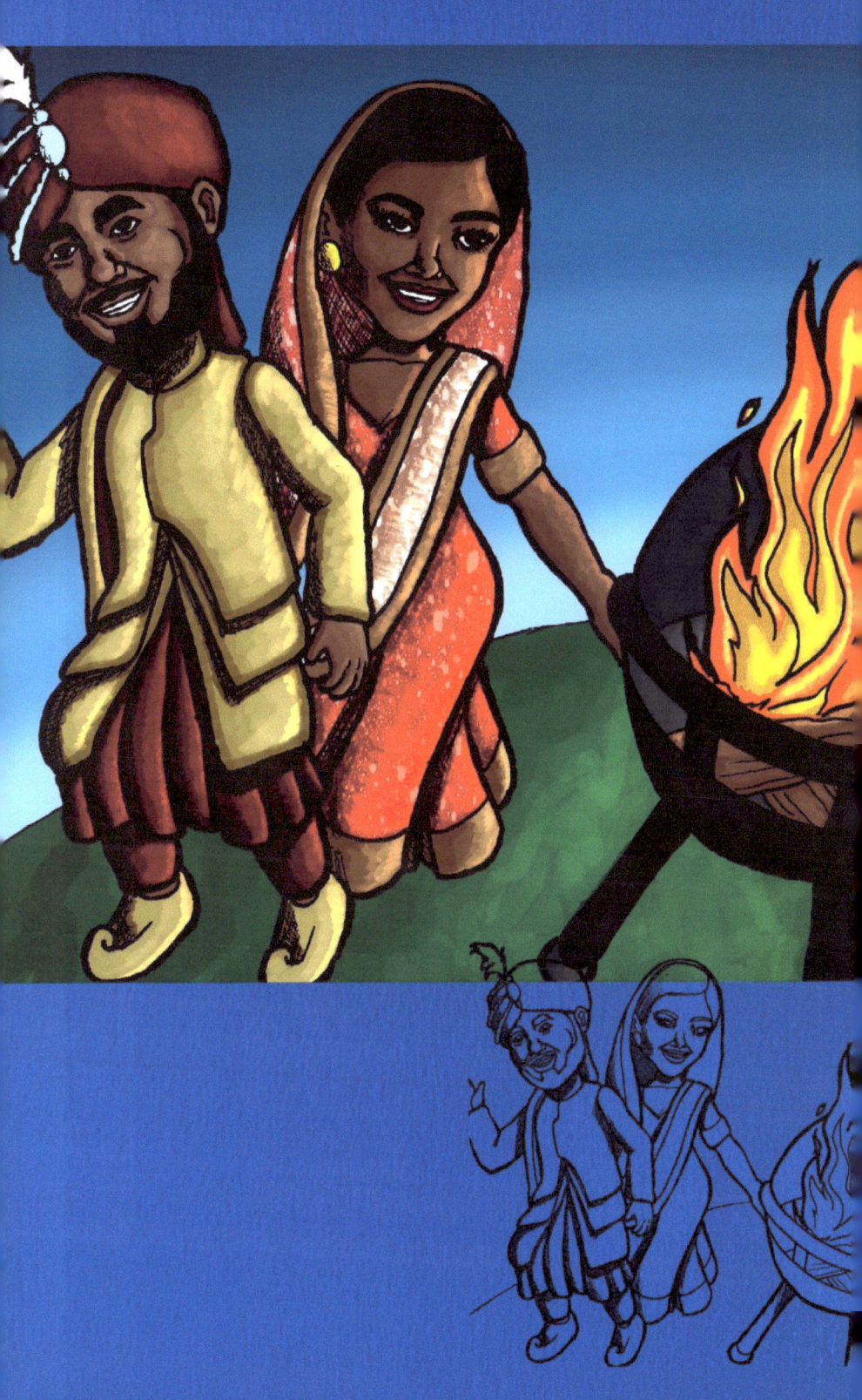

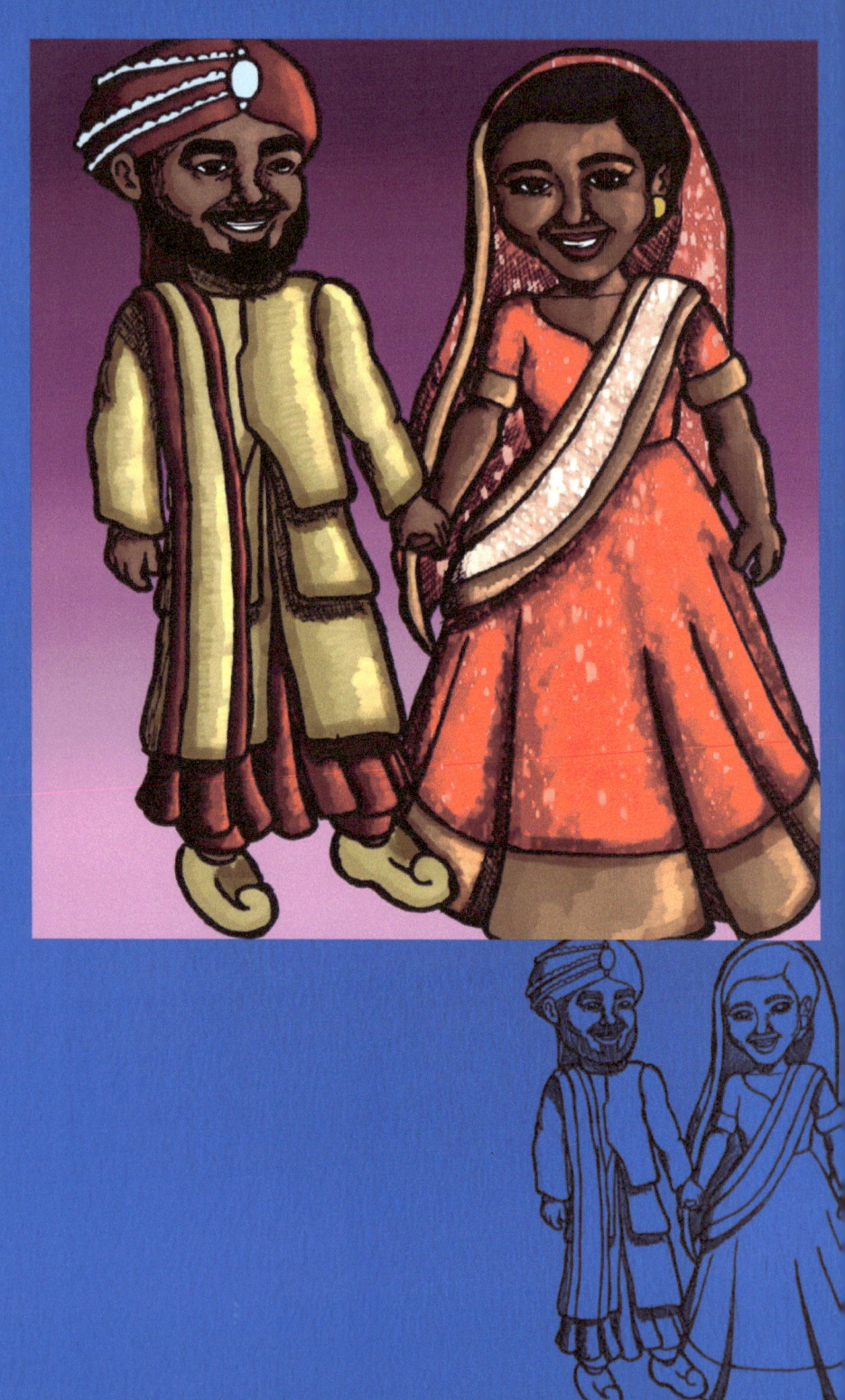

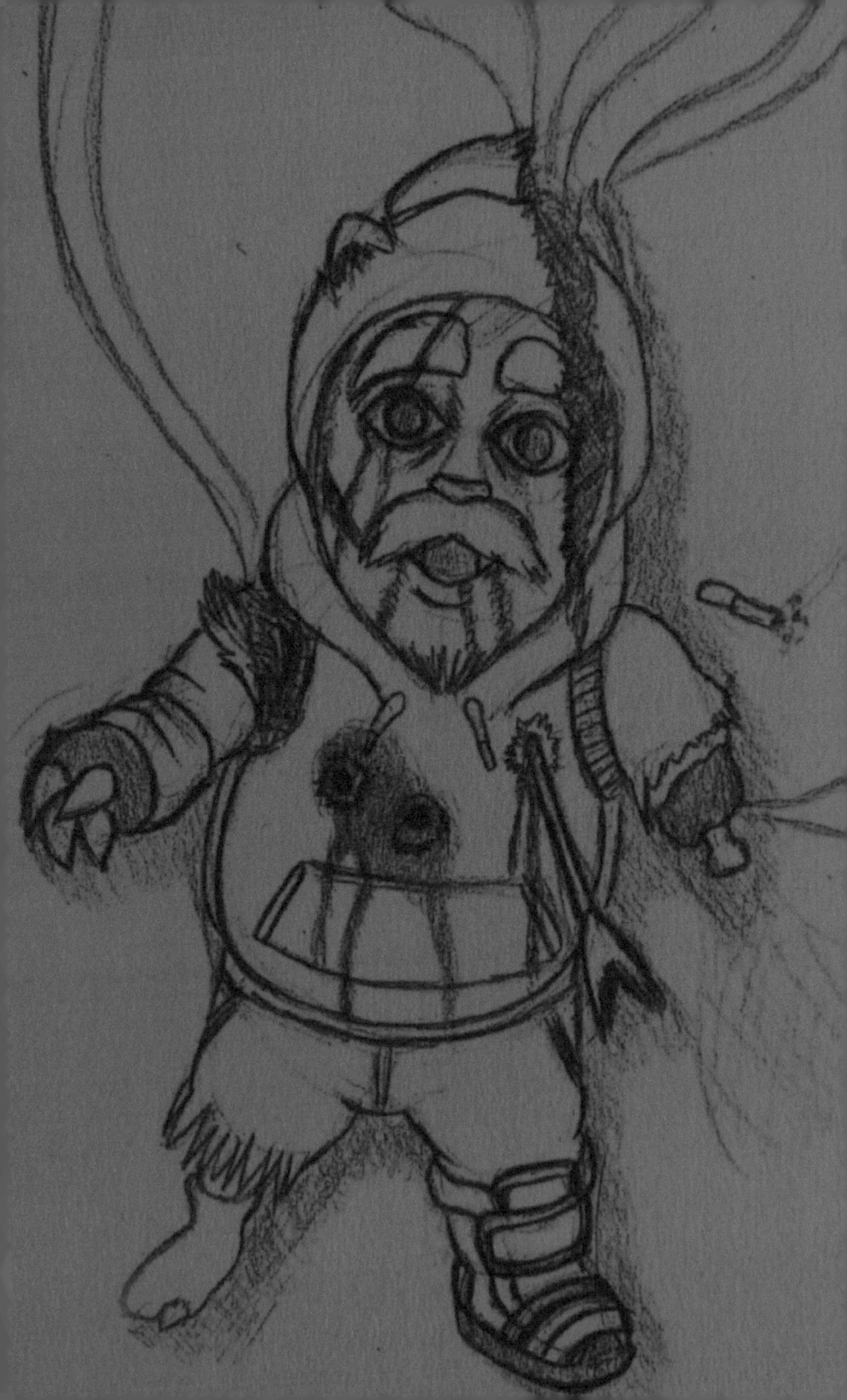

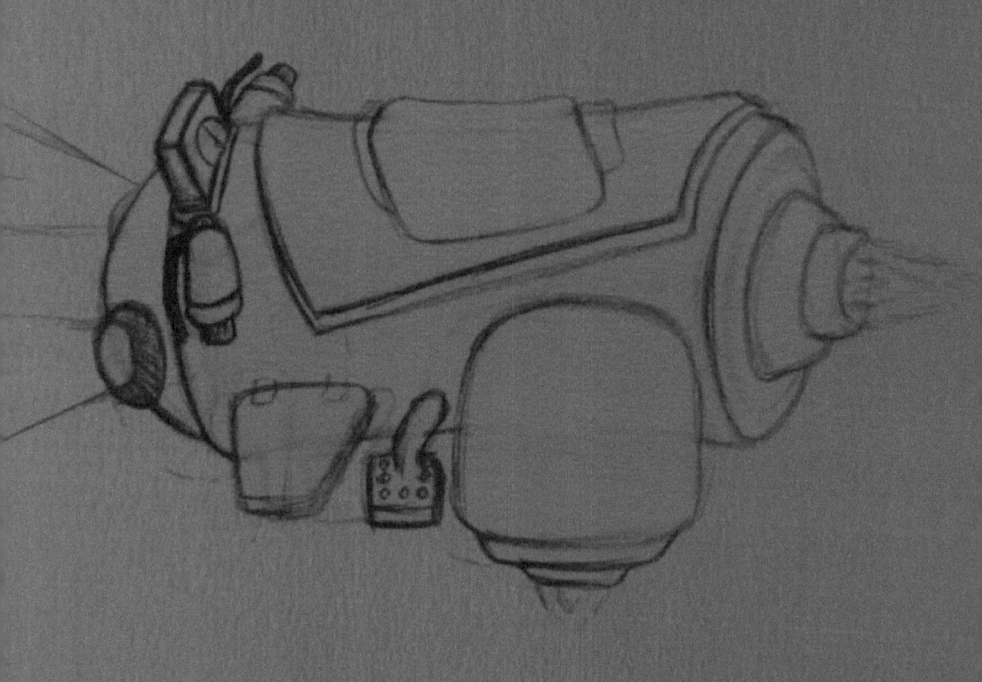

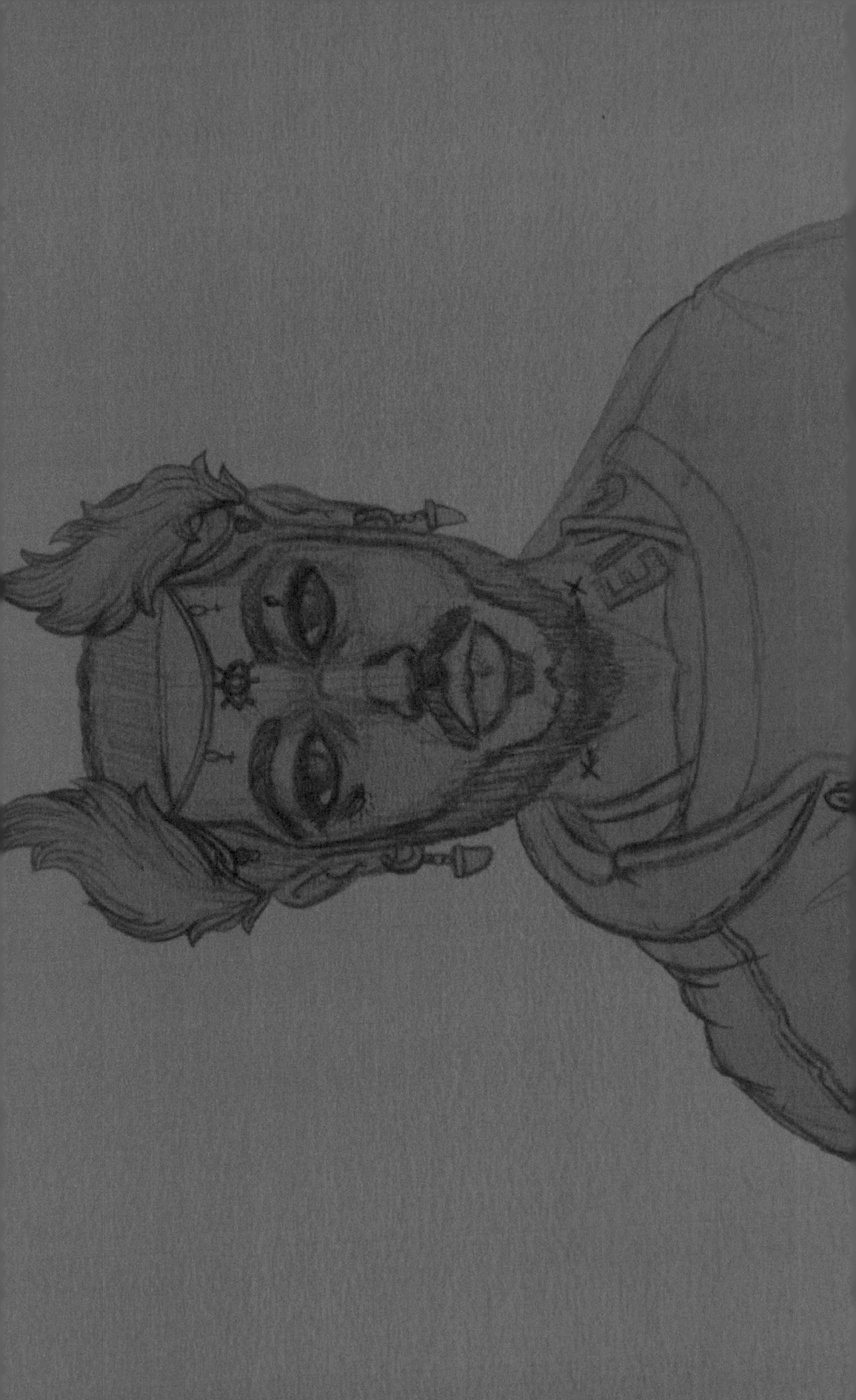

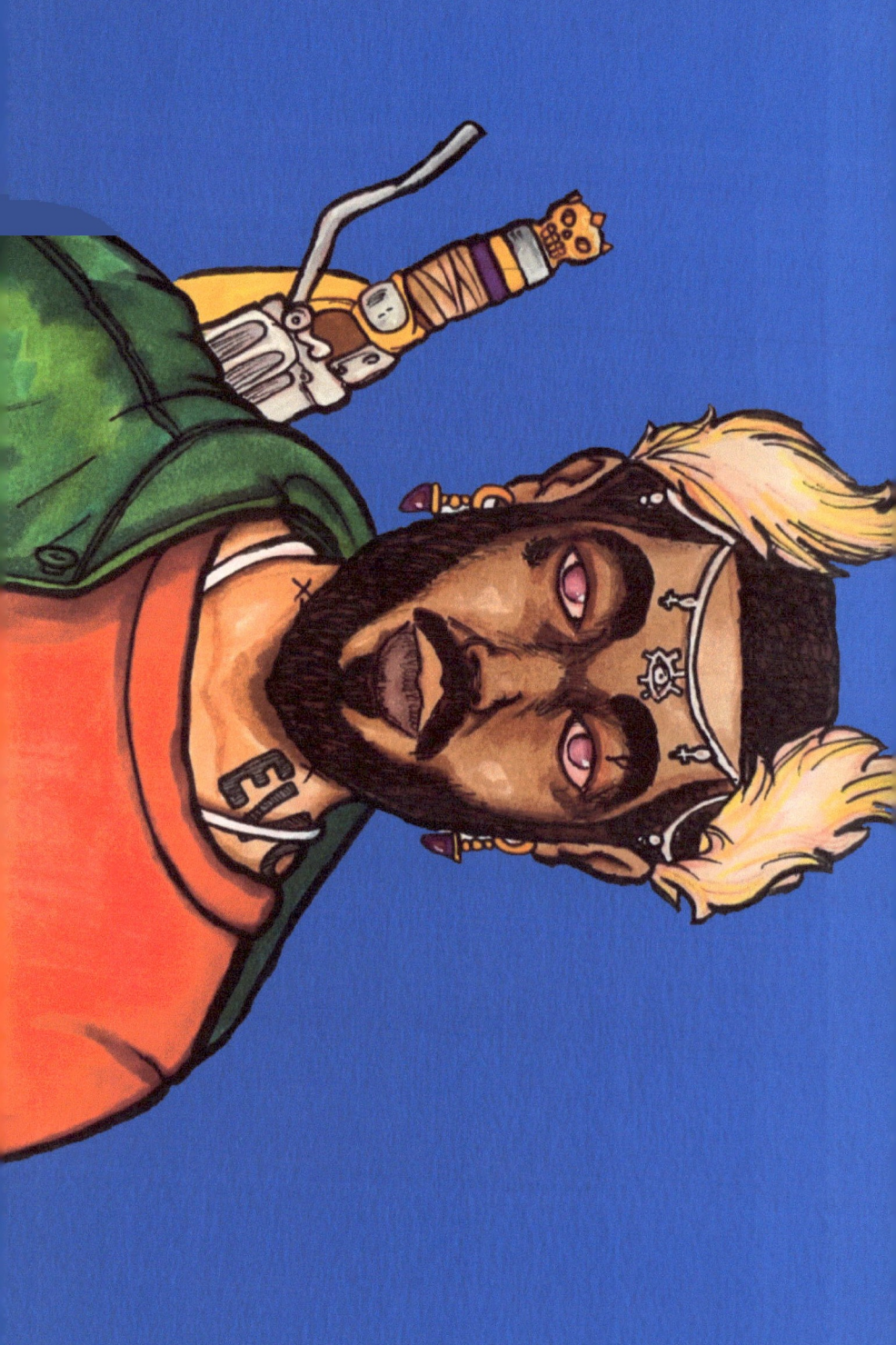

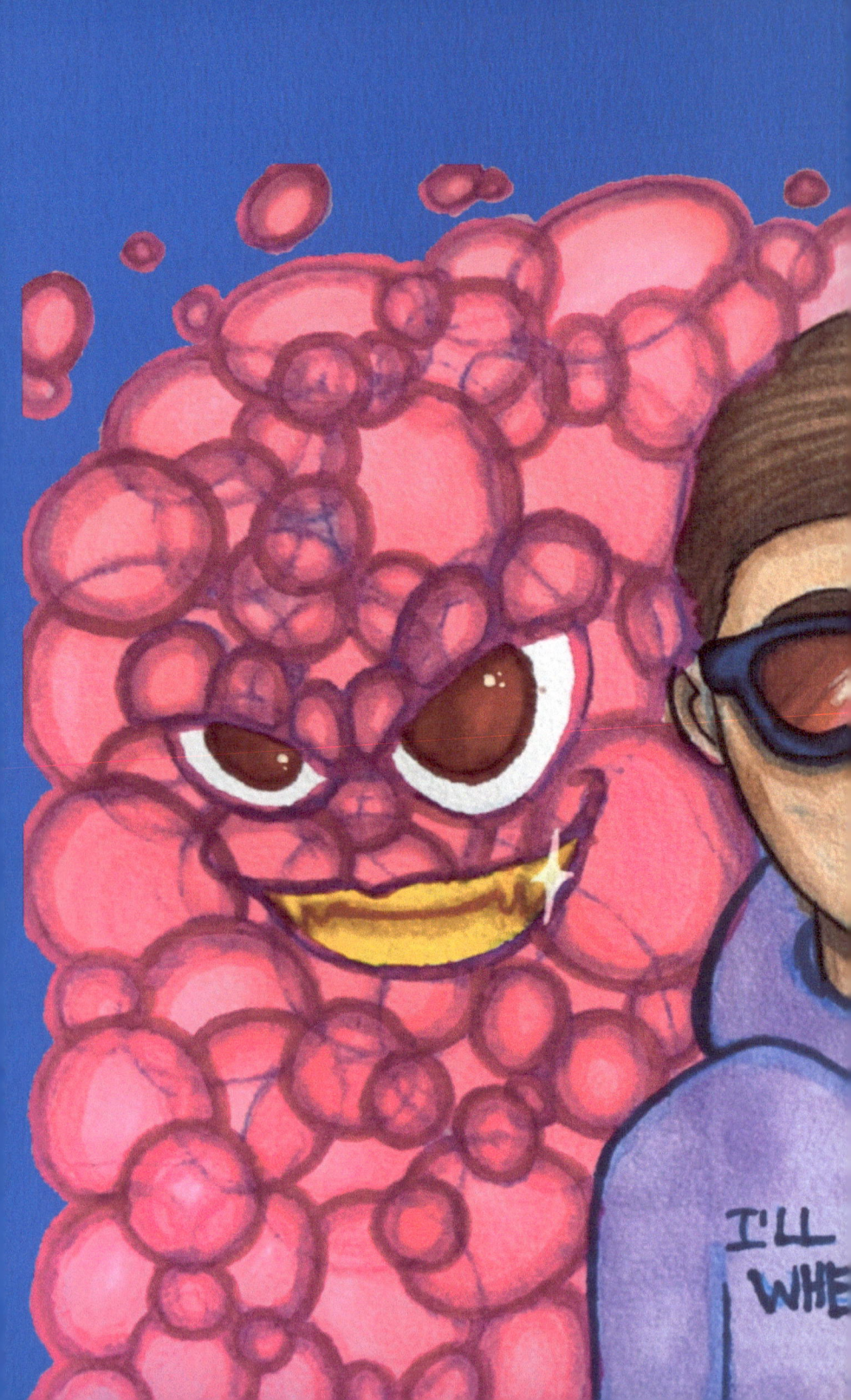

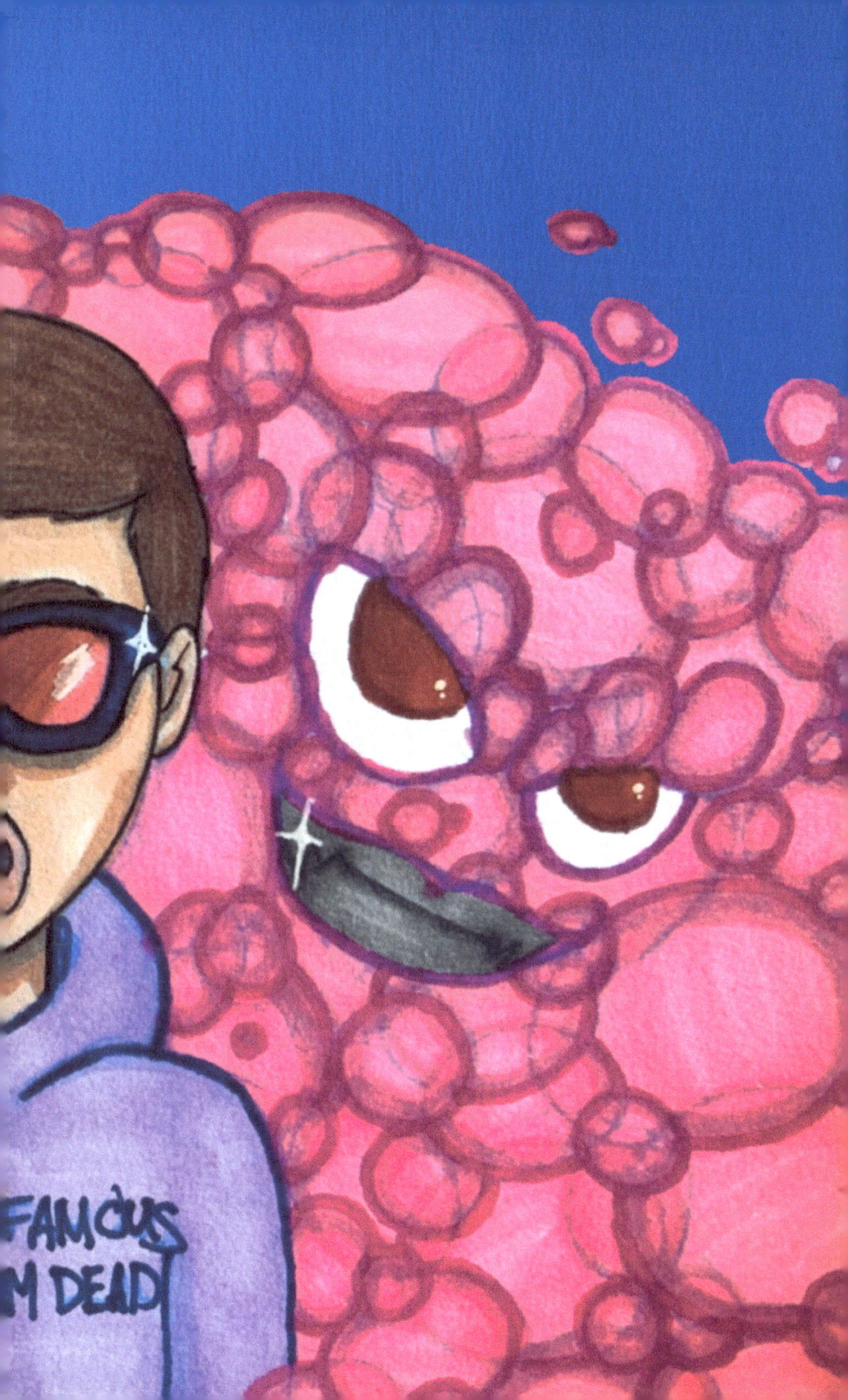

www.ingramcontent.com/pod-product-compliance
Lightning Source LLC
Chambersburg PA
CBHW040337220526
45473CB00009B/2716